I0022610

George Frederick Wright

The Glacial Boundary in Ohio, Indiana and Kentucky

George Frederick Wright

The Glacial Boundary in Ohio, Indiana and Kentucky

ISBN/EAN: 9783337125646

Printed in Europe, USA, Canada, Australia, Japan

Cover: Foto ©ninafisch / pixelio.de

More available books at **www.hansebooks.com**

The Western Reserve Historical Society,
CLEVELAND, O.

THE

GLACIAL BOUNDARY

IN OHIO,

INDIANA AND KENTUCKY.

BY

PROF. G. FREDERICK WRIGHT.

CLEVELAND, OHIO:
LEADER PRINTING COMPANY, 146 SUPERIOR STREET.
1884.

PREFACE.

WHEN, ten years ago, I began my investigations concerning the kames of the Merrimac valley, in Eastern Massachusetts, I little thought to what it would lead; and, after having traced the boundary of the glaciated area from the Atlantic Ocean to the southern part of Illinois, I am equally in doubt as to what the future has in store in this most interesting line of exploration.

The Detailed Report, occupying the larger part of the present publication, is little more than a simple recital of observations, designed to put the reader in my own position, and to furnish the facts which all scientific men would wish to know. I have endeavored to be so specific that future observers may be able to verify my statements, and may intelligently connect their own observations with mine. Whether I shall publish, in equal detail, my observations already made upon Indiana, the future must determine. I hope, however, to continue my investigations across Illinois and Missouri, and may then give fuller details of what I have already done in Indiana.

The preliminary lecture (with its map on page 17), gives the facts concerning Indiana with sufficient clearness to show their relations to those more minutely described in Ohio.

When the present report was written, I had supposed that the joint report of PROFESSOR LEWIS and myself, upon the glacial boundary in Pennsylvania, would already have appeared; and some sentences in my remarks upon Columbiana county, Ohio, presume some degree of familiarity with the views we had presented concerning what is called the "fringe" of the boundary in Western Pennsylvania. As that report will soon appear, it is not necessary to repeat here what will so soon be accessible to the public. Furthermore, my preliminary lecture puts the reader in possession of the general facts.

Among the satisfactory rewards coming to one who engages in such unremunerative, but original, investigations as those here recorded, is the ready appreciation of his work by so wide a circle of intelligent men whose time is absorbed in other occupations, but who, when the facts are brought to light, are quick to see their importance.

I have, also, had special occasion in these investigations to be thankful for the personal encouragement, appreciation, and advice of such authorities as Prof. CHARLES H. HITCHCOCK, Prof. ALPHEUS HYATT, Prof. E. S. MORSE, Prof. J. D. DANA, Prof. J. P. LESLEY, Prof. EDWARD ORTON, and Col. CHARLES WHITTLESEY. But it is to the CLEVELAND HISTORICAL SOCIETY and its friends that I am specially indebted for the means to prosecute my work in Ohio and Indiana, and that the public is indebted for so full and complete a report of the facts as is here given. The funds directly provided for my expenses, by the friends of the Society, amount to $450.00, the most of which was contributed by JARVIS M. ADAMS, Esq., President of the New York, Pennsylvania and Ohio Railroad, and Messrs. DAN P. EELLS, JOSEPH PERKINS, and T. P. HANDY. To Mr. ADAMS I am also indebted, both for passes on the railroad of which he is President, and for others secured by his intervention on the Cleveland and Pittsburgh Railway; Cleveland, Akron and Columbus; Cincinnati, Indianapolis, St. Louis and Chicago; Indianapolis and St. Louis; Ohio and Mississippi; Cleveland, Columbus, Cincinnati and Indianapolis; Pittsburgh, Cincinnati and St. Louis.

The cost of the investigations has, also, been diminished by various friends, who have accompanied me and borne their share of the expense, among whom should be mentioned Mr. J. H. KEDZIE, of Chicago, C. C. BALDWIN Esq. (Secretary of this Society, and through whose well-directed efforts the local interest in the subject is largely due), and finally the late lamented Rev. CHARLES TERRY COLLINS, whose sudden death will inflict a loss upon a multitude of philanthropic and educational enterprises. The Rev. Mr. COLLINS was first and foremost among those who set themselves to interest the Cleveland public in this matter, and he was with me two weeks in the field, entering into every minutiæ of the investigation with unbounded enthusiasm, and with sagacious appreciation of the whole bearing of the discoveries.

TABLE OF CONTENTS.

GLACIAL PERIOD IN AMERICA: PAGE.

INTRODUCTION 7

SIGNS OF GLACIATION... 9
  1. Scratches upon the Rocks.. 9
  2. Till, or Boulder Clay.. 10
  3. Transported Boulders and the Terminal Moraine.. 11
      a. Irregularity of the Boundary Line.. 11
      b. Irregular Elevation of the Boundary Line....................................... 18
      c. Character and Amount of the Debris... 21

SOME GENERAL CONSIDERATIONS.. 23
  1. Relation of the Glacial Period.. 23
      a. To Agriculture and Health.. 23
      b. To Archæology... 24
  2. Date of the Glacial Period.. 28
  3. Centers of Glacial Dispersion... 29

CONCLUSION... 31

DETAILED REPORT FOR OHIO:
COLUMBIANA COUNTY... 35
  The Fringe... 35
  The Moraine Proper... 37

STARK COUNTY... 38
  The Fringe... 38
  The Moraine Proper... 38

HOLMES COUNTY.. 43
  Berlin Township... 44
  Hardy Township.. 44
  Monroe.. 47
  Knox.. 48

KNOX COUNTY.. 49
  Jefferson Township.. 50
  Union... 50
  Butler and Jackson.. 51

LICKING COUNTY... 51
  Eden Township... 52
  Mary Ann.. 52
  Newark.. 53
  Licking and Franklin.. 53

PERRY COUNTY... 54
  Thorn Township.. 54
  Reading... 55

FAIRFIELD COUNTY... 55
  Richland and Rush Creek Townships... 56
  Pleasant.. 56
  Bern and Hocking.. 58
  Madison... 59

PICKAWAY AND HOCKING COUNTIES.. 59

6 *Contents.*

Ross County... 60
   Colerain Township.. 60
   Green... 62
   Springfield.. 63
   Union... 63
   Concord and Twin.. 64
   Buckskin and Paint.. 66
   Paxton.. 66

Pike County.. 68

Highland County.. 68
   Marshall Township... 69
   Jackson... 69

Adams County... 70

Brown Bounty... 70

Hamilton County.. 72

Kentucky... 73
   Campbell County... 73
   Kenton County... 73
   Boone County.. 74

APPENDIX:
  1. Abstract of the Bearings of Glacial Striæ and Grooves in Ohio (Compiled by
     Col. Charles Whittlesey)....................................... 77
  2. The Glacial Dam at Cincinnati.................................... 81
    a. Its Effects Along the Upper Basin of the Ohio (A Paper by Prof. I. C.
       White)... 81
    b. Its Effects in Boyd County, Ky................................ 85
    c. Mr. G. H. Squier on its effects in Bath County, Ky............ 86
    d. Prof Lesley on the Glacial Dam............................... 86

PLATES:
    I. Glaciated Region of North America.............................. 8
   II. Glaciated Region of the Delaware Valley........................ 12
  III. Glaciated Area of Pennsylvania................................ 13
  IV. Same of Ohio... 14
   V. Glacial Boundary in Indiana.................................... 17
  VI. Palæolith from France.. 24
  VII. Palæolith from New Jersey..................................... 25
 VIII. Columbiana County... 34
  IX. Stark County.. 34
   X. Holmes County... 45
  XI. Knox and Licking Counties...................................... 45
  XII. Licking, Perry, and Fairfield Counties........................ 57
 XIII. Fairfield, Hocking, Pickaway, and Ross Counties............... 57
  XIV. Ross, Pike, and Highland Counties............................. 67
  XV. Highland, Adams, and Brown Counties........................... 67
  XVI. Brown, Clermont, and Hamilton Counties........................ 71
 XVII. Kentucky... 71

A LECTURE

ON THE

GLACIAL PHENOMENA IN THE UNITED STATES,

BY

PROF. G. FREDERICK WRIGHT,

GIVEN BEFORE THE WESTERN RESERVE HISTORICAL SOCIETY,
IN CASE HALL, CLEVELAND, OHIO,
NOVEMBER 27, 1882.

NOTE.—When this lecture was delivered my investigations had reached only the Indiana line. During the present summer (1883), I have continued the exploration to the Illinois line, and hence have thought it best to make such changes in the lecture as will give the latest results.

I HAVE been led by the circumstances in which I have been placed, and which I need not here rehearse, to study somewhat extensively the glacial phenomena of the Atlantic States and of the Mississippi basin. By reason of some special familiarity with the subject, acquired by a long residence in New England, I was invited two years ago, in company with Professor H. C. Lewis, of Philadelphia, to trace the southern limits of glacial action for the Geological Survey of Pennsylvania. A full report of our work will soon appear. It is through the thoughtful generosity of several friends of this Society that I have been permitted to continue these investigations in Ohio ; and I will take this occasion to return thanks to these gentlemen and to the railroad companies who have facilitated my work. I should also say that both in this State and Pennsylvania our work has been simply supplementary to that of previous surveys. No one can appreciate more fully than myself the value of the glacial observations made by Colonel Whittlesey, Professor Newberry, Professor Orton, Professor Andrews, Mr. M. C. Read, and others of the Ohio Geological Survey. But unity could not well be given to the subject, except one person should go over the whole line, and be able to compare the phenomena of one section with those in another.

GENERAL SURVEY OF THE SUBJECT.

To understand the significance of the glacial phenomena of the State, it is necessary to take a brief survey of the general facts concerning the glacial period. A study of the phenomena of the glacial period gives one an impression of the irresistible power and grandeur of nature's operations, second only

to the study of the geological forces which elevated the conti-
nents, and to that of the astronomical forces whose effects are
seen in the motions of the heavenly bodies.   During the glacial
period more than 4,000,000 square miles of the land surface of
the Northern Hemisphere was enveloped in glacial ice.   In
North America this ice sheet extended, upon the Atlantic
coast, as far south as Long Island and New York City, and on
the Pacific coast to the southern border of British Columbia ;

PLATE I. (taken from the author's "Studies in Science and Religion ") shows a portion of the glaciated area of
North America. AA represents the boundary of the glaciated area. The continuous line is from actual survey in
1881. (For completion to Illinois, see Plates IV. and V. The broken part is still somewhat conjectural). BB marks
special glacial accumulations. UC represents Lake Agassiz, a temporary body of water formed by the damming up
by ice of the streams flowing into Hudson's Bay, the outlet being, meanwhile, through the Minnesota. D is a drift-
less region, which ice surrounded without covering. The arrows indicate the direction of glacial scratches. The
kames of New England, and the terraces upon the western rivers, are imperfectly shown upon so small a map

while in the central portion of the continent the glacier everywhere advanced nearly to the Ohio River, and in two places
crossed it. The depth of this ice-sheet in America we know
to have been at least several hundred feet at its margin, while
in the interior it was several thousand feet in depth, or deep
enough to cover the highest mountains in New England.

In Europe the land is less continuous than in America, and
hence the glacial phenomena are more difficult to interpret.
But nearly all of Ireland, the whole of Scotland, and the northern part of England and Wales show marks of long-continued
and extensive glaciation. In Switzerland the glaciers formerly
extended till they filled the whole valley between the Alps and
the Juras, and upon one side flowed down the valley of the
Rhone as far as Lyons, which is in a straight line 130 miles
from Geneva. The whole distance traversed by that portion
of the Swiss glacier was 270 miles. On the other side of the
Juras, in the valley of the Rhine, the Swiss ice-current probably met, upon the plains of Germany, the counter current
coming down from the Scandinavian peninsula; while in Italy
glaciers extended to within a short distance of the river Po, or
more than a hundred miles south of the summit of the Alps.
The Scandinavian peninsula was completely enveloped with
glacial ice, moving southerly, easterly, and westerly, in lines
of the least resistance. Upon the shores of the White Sea the
motion was nearly east and west. In Finland and in the neighborhood of Stockholm the motion was south, while upon the
west coast the motion was towards the Atlantic Ocean.

SIGNS OF GLACIATION.

The signs of glaciation are three-fold, and are unmistakable
in their meaning. These are: first, the scratches upon the
rocks ; second, the till or boulder clay ; third, the transported
boulders and terminal moraines.

FIRST. *Scratches upon the Rocks.*—All over the regions
which we have mentioned the harder and freshly uncovered
rocks show abrasion; they are polished. This, however, might
have been done by the action of water in rolling pebbles and
gravel over them. But this is not all. They are scratched and
grooved as if the sand, gravel and pebbles, which abraded them,

had been held in a firm grasp. These striæ and furrows are, in the main, parallel with each other, and they continue across the hard portions of the rock as well as the softer. There are places upon the shores, and among the Islands near the west end of Lake Erie, where many acres together of rocks, thus scratched and furrowed, are exposed, and where frequently the furrows may be traced in a continuous line for a long distance. These are effects which water alone could not produce. Water, by giving motion to pebbles, may polish the rocks over which they are moved, yet it does not give the rocks an even surface, but wears down the softer portions faster than the harder. Only moving ice is competent to produce such polishing and scratching as we have described ; and so extensive and uniform is this striation that the theory of icebergs—majestic as they are—is entirely inadequate to account for the facts.

SECOND.   *Till, or Boulder Clay.*—The competency of water for the production of the phenomena ascribed to glaciation is excluded also by the character of the superficial deposit which is everywhere found over the area indicated.   This deposit was formerly called "boulder-clay," but, in scientific circles, now goes by the name of "till," and its character is un ...istakable.

Till is an unstratified accumulation, and in this respect differs from all deposits which take place in water.   Water is a more perfect sieve than any of man's invention.   It carefully sorts whatever it transports, carrying along the finer material farther than the coarse, and depositing it by itself.   Now in the till there is no such separation of the fine from the coarse as water would secure.   Fine clay, gravel, fragments of stone of various sizes, sometimes several feet through, are mingled in one indiscriminate mass.   The larger part of the material composing till is usually derived from the rocks of the vicinity; but with this there are also mingled fragments that have been brought from a longer distance, sometimes from localities hundreds of miles away.   A noticeable peculiarity of the pebbles and fragments of rock which occur in till is that they too, like the rock beneath, are scratched, and usually the direction of the scratches on them is that of the longest diameter of the fragments.

From this description of till it will be recognized, by those who have visited the glaciers of Switzerland, as similar to the accumulation taking place beneath the glacier, and which is called the "ground moraine." In short, the fine material of the till may be compared to the dust with which a lapidary polishes his gems, and the larger fragments to the tools with which he engraves them.

THIRD. *Transported Boulders and the Terminal Moraine.* — A third evidence of the reality of the great ice movement of which we are speaking, is to be found in the character, position and limits of the transported material. This introduces us to the particular field of my own observations. There is a well-defined southern limit to the marks of glacial action in the United States. I have now followed that boundary line nearly all the way from the Atlantic Ocean to the State of Illinois, and can mark it upon the map with nearly as much confidence and accuracy as I can that of the shores of Lake Erie.

a. There are some peculiarities in this line which it is worth while to note, the first of which is the irregularity. As shown upon the maps, the boundary of the glaciated region in North America runs, opposite New England, through Nantucket and Martha's Vineyard, and forms the backbone of Long Island, entering New Jersey at Perth Amboy, just below New York.

It was my privilege, several years ago, in a more definite manner than had been done before, to call public attention to the nature of these accumulations in Southern New England. I was enabled to do this through information furnished me by Mr. Clarence King who gave me the facts in 1876, to be published in a communication to the Boston Society of Natural History upon the Glacial Phenomena of Eastern Massachusetts. (See Proceedings, Vol. 19, p. 62, 1877.) When this clew had once been furnished, it was a short matter to trace the line along the southern shore of New England and through Long Island. This work was done by Mr. Warren Upham.

By independent investigations Professors Cook and Smock, of the New Jersey Geological Survey, discovered the significance of certain glacial accumulations in that State, and a little later published (Report on the Geology of New Jersey for 1878)

a map of the Terminal Moraine in New Jersey. This runs by
au irregular course from Perth Amboy to Belvidere, on the
Delaware River, a few miles above Easton.

PLATE 11. (taken from "Studies in Science and Religion") shows, in addition to the
glaciated area of New Jersey, the glacial terraces of gravel along the Lehigh and Delaware
Rivers, and also the "Delta Terrace" at Trenton, fifty feet above the river, in which Dr. C.
C. Abbott has found palæolithic implements. (For cuts, see Plates VI. and VII., pp. 24, 25)

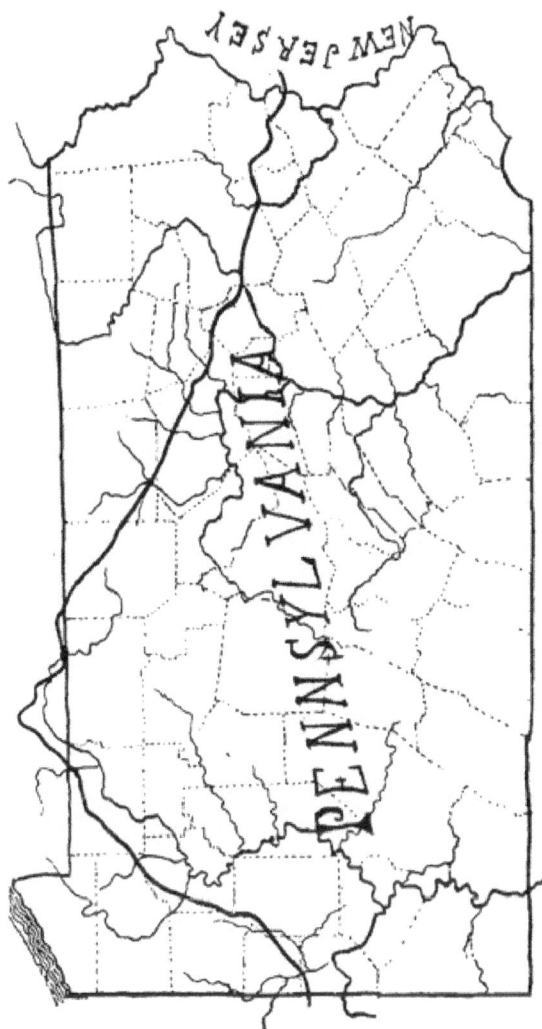

PLATE III. The broad, black line shows Southern Boundary of Glaciated Area of Pennsylvania.

From that point the line runs in a general northwesterly direction to the vicinity of Salamanca, N. Y., and thence southwesterly into Boone county, Ky., across the river from Cincinnati. Thence, by a circuitous route, hereafter to be de-

scribed, it passes to the southwest corner of Indiana. So far
it has been accurately traced. From geological reports we
suppose it to trend across Illinois into Missouri, and thence in
a more northerly course into the States and Territories beyond.
Taken in their full extent, the curves in this boundary line
are both graceful and majestic, and may yet furnish to the
mathematician some clew as to the depth of the ice and the
distance of the centers from which it was dispersed. Various
minor curves in the line are also worthy of notice, one of which
appears in New Jersey, where near Rockaway the line makes
a right angle. One or two graceful curves are also noticeable
between the Delaware and Susquehanna rivers. Near Sala-

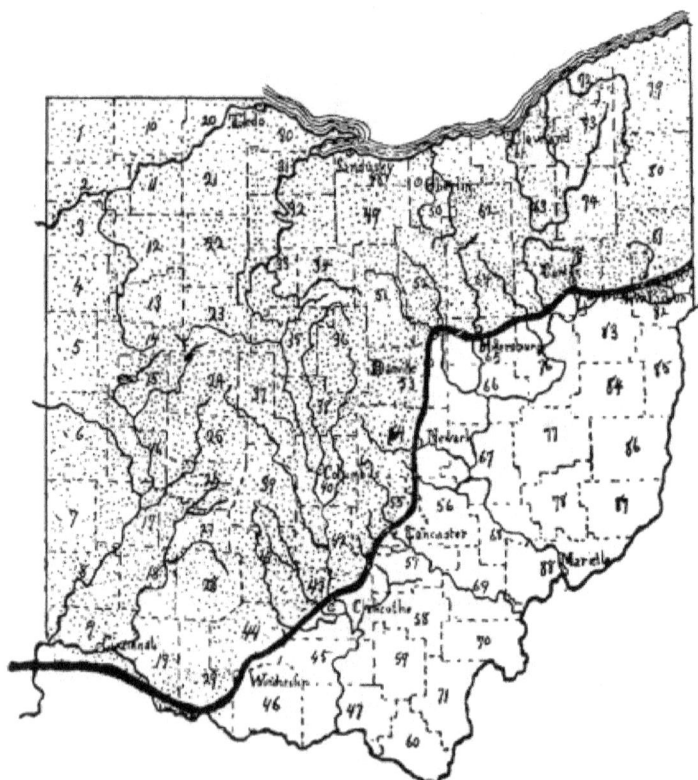

PLATE IV. Map showing Southern Boundary of Glaciated Area of Southern Ohio.

LIST OF COUNTIES WITH NUMBERS CORRESPONDING TO THOSE IN MAP.

No. I.

1. Williams.	23. Hardin.	45. Pike.	67. Muskingum.
2. Defiance.	24. Logan.	46. Adams.	68. Morgan.
3. Paulding.	25. Champaign.	47. Scioto.	69. Athens.
4. Van Wert.	26. Clarke.	48. Erie.	70. Meigs.
5. Mercer.	27. Greene.	49. Huron.	71. Gallia.
6. Darke.	28. Clinton.	50. Lorain.	72. Lake.
7. Preble.	29. Brown.	51. Richland.	73. Geauga.
8. Butler.	30. Ottawa.	52. Ashland.	74. Portage.
9. Hamilton.	31. Sandusky.	53. Knox.	75. Stark.
10. Fulton.	32. Seneca.	54. Licking.	76. Tuscarawas.
11. Henry.	33. Wyandot.	55. Fairfield.	77. Guernsey.
12. Putnam.	34. Crawford.	56. Perry.	78. Noble.
13. Allen.	35. Marion.	57. Hocking.	79. Ashtabula.
14. Auglaize.	36. Morrow.	58. Vinton.	80. Trumbull.
15. Shelby.	37. Union.	59. Jackson.	81. Mahoning.
16. Miami.	38. Delaware.	60. Lawrence.	82. Columbiana.
17. Montgomery.	39. Madison.	61. Cuyahoga.	83. Carroll.
18. Warren.	40. Franklin.	62. Medina.	84. Harrison.
19. Clermont.	41. Fayette.	63. Summit.	85. Jefferson.
20. Lucas.	42. Pickaway.	64. Wayne.	86. Belmont.
21. Wood.	43. Ross.	65. Holmes.	87. Monroe.
22. Hancock.	44. Highland.	66. Coshocton.	88. Washington.

No. II.

Adams................46	Hamilton................9	Noble....................,78
Allen.................,13	Hancock................22	Ottawa 30
Ashland(1242 ft. ab. sea level).52	Hardin (1371)............23	Paulding 3
Ashtabula 79	Harrison (1180).........84	Perry (1156)............56
Athens................69	Henry....................11	Pickaway.................42
Auglaize................14	Highland (1135).........44	Pike (1285)..............45
Belmont (1170).........86	Hocking................57	Portage (1260)............74
Brown.................29	Holmes (1235)..........65	Preble (1044)............. 7
Butler.................. 8	Huron (1050)............49	Putnam...............12
Carroll (1011). 83	Jackson................59	Richland (1400)...........51
Champaign (1158)......25	Jefferson (1065)..........85	Ross..................43
Clarke.................26	Knox (1295)............53	Sandusky...............31
Clermont............ ...19	Lake (1175)..............72	Scioto..................47
Clinton (1095)..........28	Lawrence................60	Seneca ... .32
Columbiana (1419)......82	Licking (1316)...........54	Shelby (1058)............15
Coshocton (1326).......66	Logan (1550)............24	Stark (1261).............75
Crawford (1175).........34	Lorain................50	Summit (1175)............63
Cuyahoga (1032). 61	Lucas 20	Trumbull (1165)..........80
Darke (1107)............ 6	Madison 39	Tuscarawas (1491)..........76
Defiance................ 2	Mahoning (1208).........81	Union..................37
Delaware............ ...38	Marion................35	Van Wert................ 4
Erie 48	Medina (1117)...........62	Vinton.................58
Fairfield 55	Meigs....................70	Warren.................18
Fayette.............,...41	Mercer................ 5	Washington..............88
Franklin 40	Miami................16	Wayne (1275)............64
Fulton 10	Monroe................87	Williams.................. 1
Gallia.................71	Montgomery............17	Wood..................21
Geauga (12 2)..........73	Morgan................68	Wyandot................33
Greene................27	Morrow (1148)..........36	
Guernsey...............77	Muskingum (1161).......67	

manca, in New York, the change of direction is such as to
make an acute angle. Omitting various other deflections in
Pennsylvania, you will notice several of a very marked character in Ohio.

The boundary line enters Ohio near Palestine, in Columbiana county, and crosses the county in a direction a little
south of west, and as it enters Stark county, trends a little
to the north as far as Canton. Here it makes a sharp turn,
and runs almost south to the edge of Tuscarawas county,
entering Holmes county near its northeast corner, and continuing in a southwesterly course to Millersburg, whence it trends
northwesterly to the southern township of Ashland county,
where it again takes a very sudden and decided turn to the
south, passing through the eastern edge of Knox county;
thence through Newark, in Licking county, to the reservoir
in the northwestern part of Perry county, continuing in its
southerly course to Rushville in Fairfield county. Thence it
bends rapidly westward to Lancaster, and again, after crossing
the Hocking Valley, turns southward and runs along the boundary between Pickaway and Hocking counties to Adelphi, in
the northeast corner of Ross county. Here again it bends
westward, crossing the Scioto Valley a few miles above Chillicothe, turning again southward, near Frankfort, and bending
around so as to just graze the northwest corner of Pike county,
and cross the southeastern of Highland and the northwestern
of Adams, entering Brown county near Decatur, and running westward across the southern townships of Brown and
Clermont counties, and crossing the Ohio River into Kentucky
about two miles north of the line between Campbell and Pendleton counties, whence it bends northward, keeping nearly
parallel with the river, and from three to eight miles south of
it, re-crossing the river near Woolpers Creek, five miles south
of Petersburg, and entering Indiana a little below Aurora.

In Indiana, the line still continues to bear in a southerly
direction through Ohio and Jefferson counties, grazing the edge
of Kentucky again opposite Madison and reaching its southern-
most point near Charleston in Clarke county, Indiana. From
here it bears again to the north through Scott and Jackson

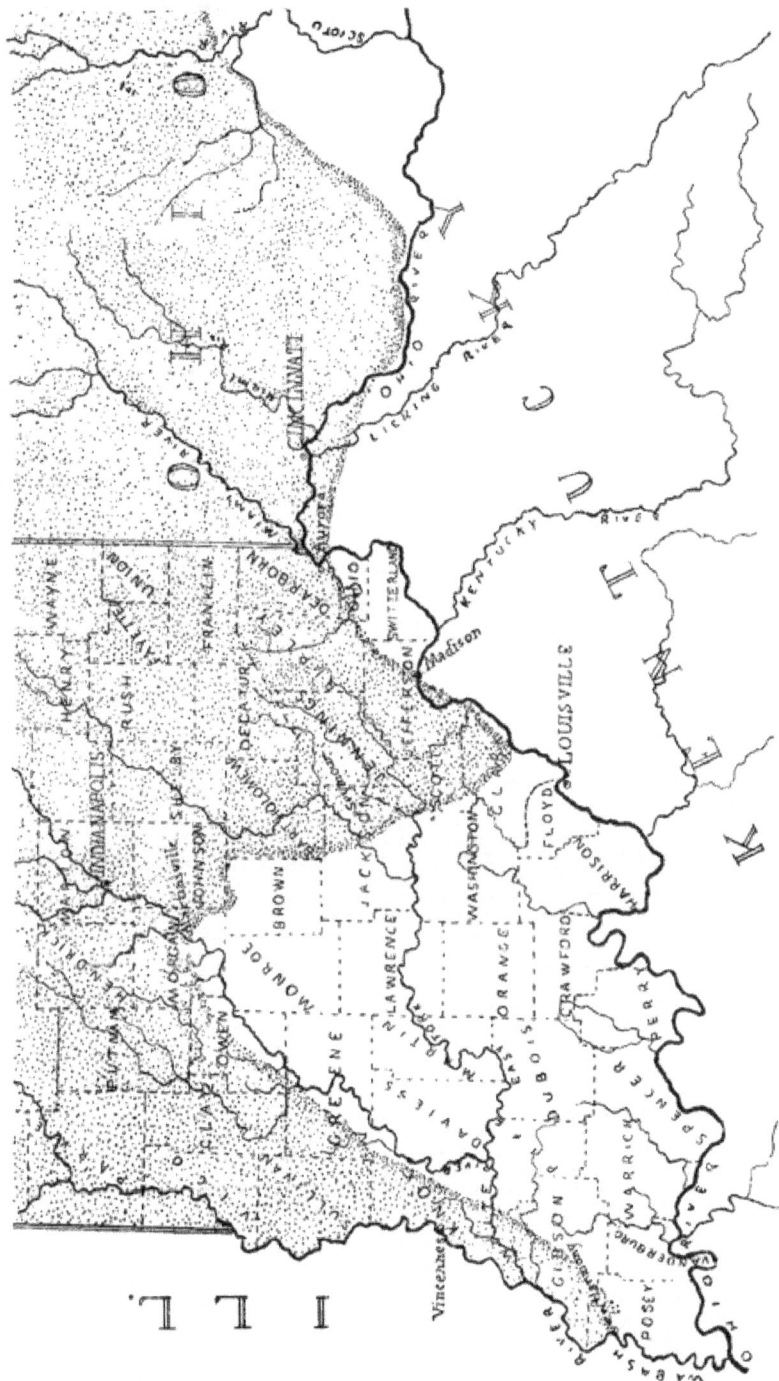

PLATE V. Map of Southern Indiana, showing Glacial Boundary.

counties to the line between Bartholomew and Brown, and follows this to the northeast corner of Brown. There again it turns to the southwest, touching the northeast corner of Monroe, where it again bears north for ten miles, to near Martinsville in Morgan county. Here again the line turns west and south, passing diagonally through Owen, Greene, Knox, and Gibson counties, and into Posey county as far as New Harmony, where, for the present, I have left it.

To account for these curves is a problem to which we will return a little later.

b. A second class of peculiarities to be noted in this boundary line is its irregularity as to elevation. Nowhere is there manifest any barrier such as would limit a body of water, and the line rises over mountains and descends into the valleys with apparent indifference. South of New England the accumulations forming the terminal moraine are often below the level of the sea,—the Elizabeth Islands and Block Island being merely the surface of the moraine where it is partly buried in the ocean ; so on across Long Island, Staten Island, and a good part of New Jersey, the moraine is not far above the level of the sea. West of the Delaware the line mounts the summit of the Blue Ridge, 1,500 feet above the sea, and descends in crossing a transverse valley, a few miles to the north, 1,000 feet. It ascends again, in a few more miles, the summit of Pocono Mountain, which forms the watershed between the Delaware and the Lehigh, and is 2,000 feet above the sea. Upon reaching the east branch of the Susquehanna at Beech Haven, it has again descended 1,500 feet, and it keeps on in a nearly uniform course until it mounts the escarpment of the Alleghanies north of Williamsport. From this point on to Salamanca the elevation varies from 2,000 to 2,500 feet. Once across the Alleghanies the line works gradually to a lower level until it reaches the southern part of Ohio, where it is still nearly 1,000 feet above the sea.

These facts by themselves clearly show that the boundary line which we have traced, does not, as Dr. Dawson supposes, mark the shores of an ancient sea, for if that were the case, there would have been a barrier to limit the sea, and that barrier must have been upon the same general level, which, as we have seen, is not the case.

Nor have there been any physical changes since the glacial period sufficient to produce these diversities of elevation. The Alleghanies were uplifted millions of years before the glacial period. This is evident from the immense amount of erosion which had taken place before the glacial period. Southeastern Ohio and Western Pennsylvania are covered with the strata of the coal measures, some outlying fragments of which are still to be found as far east as the Susquehanna Valley. Now the rivers in all this region flow along the bottoms of deep troughs almost like canons, which in the course of ages have been cut down by water through the parallel strata of sandstone, lime, shale, and coal, which, in alternate layers, built up the great structure of the carboniferous period. The extent and depth of these narrow valleys of erosion are scarcely appreciated. For fifty miles above Lock Haven, in Pennsylvania, the Philadelphia and Erie Railway follows up a narrow winding gorge, in the west branch of the Susquehanna, which is 1,000 feet in depth. Instead of digging for the coal in this region they ascend the summits of the hills. The Allegheny and the Ohio rivers occupy similar troughs, which are from 300 to 500 feet in depth. These are valleys of erosion, and every tributary of these streams occupies a similar trough which it has cut for itself. It is certain that the main lines of drainage upon this continent do not now differ materially from those which have existed from the very earliest time.

I say *materially*, because in minor respects the glaciation of the continent produced many permanent changes in the drainage, and, for a temporary period, changes that were remarkable. But, in the main, the watershed between the St. Lawrence and the Mississippi has been, from the coal period on, a well-defined and permanent feature in the physical geography of the United States. The minor changes in the drainage of this country have been largely due to the work of the glacial period. Everywhere over the glaciated region the till, or ground moraine, has been forced like putty into the gorges formed by the erosion of pre-glacial streams, so that nothing is more common throughout this region than to find that the old channels have been buried, and the streams forced to flow in new channels of modern date.

  c. A third peculiarity in the border of the glaciated region is the character and amount of the accumulations marking it. Along a considerable portion of this boundary line the accumulations of glaciated material are immense. South of New England the boundary is marked by a line of hills from 50 to 250 feet in height, and from two to three miles wide. These hills are composed of loose material, thrown together in irregular hummocks and ridges, with many enclosed depressions to which there are no outlets, and which, from their shape, are called "kettle-holes." Many large boulders, brought from a long distance, are found scattered over these hummocks. There can be no question that this is a terminal moraine, marking the line from east to west, along which the ice-front rested for a considerable period, and where, from century to century, it deposited the burdens of rock and earth which it had picked up in its journey from the north. This was the line of battle between the frosts of the north and the tropical winds of the south. Here, as the sun melted back the ice in summer, the ice deposited its earthy material, and in the winter regained its ground to repeat the process and beat a retreat the following summer, and so on until these immense hills had been deposited. In New England we can often trace the boulders to ledges scores of miles to the north. Across New Jersey these moraine hills continue upon a corresponding scale. West of New Jersey the broken and mountainous character of the country has frequently disguised the facts, so that they are somewhat more difficult of discovery. But even here the genuine features of a terminal moraine reappear so often that there can be no question about the mode of its formation. We may note especially a remarkable development of moraine hills upon the level summit of Pocono Mountain. Here, for many miles, and 2,000 feet above the sea, are almost exactly repeated the features which we have described in Southern New England. One may travel from the southward for a long distance, over

an elevated plain whose only covering of soil is a foot or two of
sand and angular fragments arising from the sub-aerial disintegration of the underlying level strata of Pocono sandstone;
when suddenly, near Tobyhanna, he intersects the majestic
curve of moraine hills just referred to. Down to this limit
glaciated stones are piled in every imaginable confusion. Here,
in dense forests, are kettle-holes, many of which are still filled
with water, which slowly drains away through the loose material near the rim.   Here, in the *debris* which goes to form
these hills, are granite boulders which must be hundreds of
miles away from their native place.

Omitting for the present further reference to Pennsylvania
and coming to Ohio, we find in Columbiana county and the
eastern part of Stark county, that the accumulation of glacial
material along the front of the ice, is somewhat less marked in
quantity than farther east, but is the same in quality.   The
apparent diminution in quantity may arise from its having
been spread over a wider base.   But, near the western part of
Columbiana county, at New Alexandria, two or three miles
back from the very extreme limit of glacial signs, the familiar
knobs and kettle-holes of the moraine are distinctly marked,
and that upon the very height of the land.   Wells are here
sunk from thirty to fifty feet without passing through the glacial accumulation.   A mile or two west of Canton, in Stark
county, the accumulations of glaciated material are upon a
scale equal to anything in New England.   The northern part
of Holmes county is covered with till which is everywhere of
great depth, and in numerous places near the margin displays,
though in a moderate degree, the familiar inequalities of the
New England moraine.   After the southern deflection in Knox
county, the glaciated region is entered near Danville, from the
east, on the Columbus, Mt. Vernon & Akron Railroad, through
a cut in till a quarter of a mile long, and from thirty to forty
feet in depth.   At the old village of Danville near by upon a
neighboring hill, wells are reported as descending more than a
hundred feet without reaching the bottom of the till.   Through
Licking county, both north and south of Newark, the depth
of the glacial envelope is great up to within a short distance of

its eastern edge. At the reservoir in Perry county the distinct features of a moraine come out. The hill upon which Thornville is built is a mass of glaciated material in which wells descend from thirty to fifty feet without striking rock. This is upon the highest land of the vicinity. The reservoir itself seems to be in a great kettle-hole or moraine basin. All through Fairfield county the glacial accumulation is of a great depth down to a very short distance of its margin. But perhaps the most remarkable of all the portions of this line in Ohio is that running from Adelphi, in the northeast corner of Ross county, to the Scioto River. The accumulation at Adelphi is more than two hundred feet, and continues at this height for many miles westward. Riding along upon its uneven summit, one finds the surface strewn with granite boulders, and sees stretching off to the northwest the magnificent and fertile plains of Pickaway county, while close to the south of him, yet marked by a distinct interval, are the cliffs of Waverley sandstone rising two hundred or three hundred feet higher, which here and onward to the south pretty closely approach the boundary of the glaciated region.

Passing over the intervening space, we note that in Boone county, Kentucky, the accumulation of glacial material extends several miles south of the Ohio River, and many feet in depth, and is here at an elevation of more than 500 feet above the river. At an equal elevation similar accumulations appear across the river in Indiana, west of Lawrenceburg,

At every step along the line, as thus traced through Ohio' granitic boulders of every size and shape and complexion are to be found. The two largest measured were one in Columbiana county, near Hanovertown, which is thirteen feet long by eleven feet wide, and which stands eight feet out of the ground; and another near Lancaster, in Fairfield county, which is eighteen feet long, twelve feet wide, and stands six feet out of ground. These are granite boulders, whose native ledges are in Canada, far to the north of Lake Erie. Boulders from three feet to five feet in diameter are too numerous to mention.

SOME GENERAL CONCLUSIONS.

Several interesting subsidiary considerations are connected with this subject:

FIRST. *The Glacial Period and the Interests of Agriculture and Health.*—In this State, and probably further west, the prairie region is seen to have been a product of the glacial period. It was the moving ice of that period which wore down the prominences and filled up the depressions to produce the dead level or gently rolling surface of all this prairie region. The action of running streams produces fertile intervales in narrow valleys, but the sheet of ice that pressed over our continent ground up the rocks, and spread the *detritus* over the whole surface. In the level regions of the West the soil is nearly everywhere fertile. A noticeable quality in the soil of the glaciated region is the mixture of the elements composing it. All the rocks to the north have contributed to its composition. In the soil of Lorain county, for example, there are found the pulverized fragments of various granites from Canada, of the limestones of the Sandusky group, mingled with those of the neighboring shales and sandstones. All these elements have been kneaded together into one homogeneous mass by the moving ice, as the housewife kneads her flour and yeast together.

The legislators of the State do not yet fully appreciate the economical and sanitary bearings of glacial investigations. The ice movement of the glacial period pretty much made the inhabitable portions of this State. It determined the character of the soil, the contour of the country, the minor lines of drainage, and thus in a thousand ways had to do with the pleasure, the health, and the prosperity of the present population. As, a few weeks ago, I marked off the glacial limits on a map of this State, the Secretary of the Board of Agriculture at once remarked to me that that was the southern boundary of the great wheat-producing portion of the State, and expressed an earnest desire that Ohio might secure as thorough an examination of the glacial phenomena within its bounds as has been done by New Jersey. Certainly if one is to buy a farm in Ohio he should pray that it be either in a river valley or north of the terminal moraine. Of course this is to be taken as a general statement, to which there are exceptions; but even then it will be found that the exception proves the rule.

SECOND. *Relation to Archæology.*—Dr. C. C. Abbott reports that he has found palæolithic implements (one of which is shown in the accompanying cut, together with one from France for comparison) stratified with the gravel forming the terrace of the Delaware River, at Trenton, N. J. I have repeatedly visited that place with Dr. Abbott, and in company

PLATE VI. The palæolith here shown is natural size, and is No. 3034 of the Mortillet collection from Abbeville, France. The geological conditions under which this was found are very similar to those of the palæolith from Trenton, N. J.

PLATE VII. This palæolith is shortened one inch in the cut, and is proportionally narrow, the original being 5 6-8 inches long and 8 1-8 wide. This is No. 19723 in Dr. Abbott's collection from Trenton, N. J. The Mortillet and Dr. Abbott's collections are both in the Archæological Museum, in Cambridge, Mass., where these specimens can at any time be seen. No 19723 is specially interesting, because Professor Putnam took it with his own hands out of Trenton gravel from behind a small boulder which was firmly embedded four feet below the surface of the soil. (See Proceedings of Boston Society of Natural History, Vol. XXI , p. 149.) For the geological condition, see Plate II., p. 12; for a more detailed account, see "Studies in Science and Religion," Chapter VI.

with Professor Dawkins of England and Professor H. W. Haynes of Boston,—two of the highest authorities upon palæolithic implements that can be found in the world,—and they testify that the implements found by Dr. Abbott, both in their form and in the situations in which they occur, closely correspond to those which have been so carefully studied in northern France and southern England.

An examination of the terraces along the Delaware at once brings these implements into definite relation to the glacial period. The gravel in which they are found is glacial gravel deposited upon the banks of the Delaware when, during the last stages of the glacial period, the river was swollen with vast floods of water from the melting ice. Man was on this continent at that period when the climate and ice of Greenland extended to the mouth of New York harbor. The probability is that if he was in New Jersey at that time he was also upon the banks of the Ohio, and the extensive terrace and gravel deposits in the southern part of our State should be closely scanned by archæologists. When observers become familiar with the rude form of these palæolithic implements they will doubtless find them in abundance. But whether we find them or not in this State, if you admit, as I am compelled to do, the genuineness of those found by Dr. Abbott, our investigations into the glacial phenomena of Ohio must have an important archæological significance, for they bear upon the question of the chronology of the glacial period, and so upon that of man's appearance in New Jersey.

To appreciate the bearing of glacial studies upon this question we must return to study the old water courses which existed in glacial times. As you can see, a special interest attaches to those rivers which rise in the glaciated region and in the lower part of their course flow through the unglaciated. Man lived first below the glacial limit, and fished upon the banks of the streams which were periodically gorged with the spring freshets of the glacial period, and during those floods lost his spear-heads, his hammers, his axes and scrapers, where they became mingled with the gravel brought down from up the stream. The Delaware River happens to be the first stream west of the

Atlantic whose source is in the glaciated region and whose mouth is in the unglaciated. But, in following the terminal moraine westward, we are continually crossing streams which are similarly situated; such are, in Pennsylvania, the Lehigh, the east branch of the Susquehanna, the various creeks which empty into the west branch of the Susquehanna, and those which empty into the Allegheny River; all of which, I can testify from personal inspection, substantially repeat in their terrace formations the phenomena along the Delaware River, where it passes from the glaciated to the unglaciated region. Where these streams emerge from the glacial region there are uniformly immense deposits of granitic pebbles and coarse gravel, and, for long distances below, terraces of finer gravel far above the present high-water mark.

Ohio abounds in streams similarly situated, among which may be mentioned the forks of the Beaver and Sandy Creeks, in Columbiana county; the Nimishillin, the Tuscarawas, and Sugar Creek, in Stark county; the Killbuck and Mohican, in Holmes county; the Licking, in Licking county; Jonathan Creek, in Perry county; the Hocking River and Muddy Prairie Run, in Fairfield county; and Salt Creek, the Scioto, and the forks of Paint Creek, in Ross county. To this list may also be added the Ohio itself.

The Ohio is in every respect unique in its relations to the glacial period. Through the whole of its course from Pittsburg to Cairo, it is, roughly speaking, parallel with the terminal moraine, and all along its course has received from the north the contributions of water and ice and gravel which poured down from the decaying ice-front but a short distance away. And now the discovery of glacial deposits in Campbell and Boone counties, Kentucky, adds another exceedingly interesting feature to the problem. Here, as we have seen, the ice actually crossed and projected several miles south of the Ohio River. From the elevation at which these accumulations occur it is certain that the ice-barrier at Cincinnati must have been at least six hundred feet. This would set the water of the Ohio beyond Pittsburg, far up into the Allegheny and Monongahela rivers, submerging Pittsburg itself to a depth of about three hundred feet. This discovery helps to explain some facts observed a year ago in our survey of the moraine in Pennsylvania. We shall expect to find this theory verified by a variety of observations upon the upper course of the Ohio and its tributaries. We shall expect to find also, in Kentucky, some indications of the outlet of this temporary glacial lake.

It is interesting to reproduce by the imagination the form and appearance of this lake. The barrier probably was not high enough to submerge all the highlands of southeastern Ohio, or of northern Kentucky and of West Virginia; but long bays must have stretched up on the north through all the valleys to the ice-front. Thus the glacier in southeastern Ohio would for awhile seem to terminate in an archipelago. How long this condition of things existed it is impossible to tell with certainty, but from the limited amount of the deposit south of the Ohio River a relatively brief period is indicated. The Ohio Valley, both before and after the formation of this ice-barrier, must have presented inviting haunts for palæolithic man. It is of the utmost importance to archæology that the gravels of this valley should be carefully scanned. Probably there is nowhere in the world so inviting a field for such investigation as the banks of the Ohio and its tributaries.

THIRD. *Date of the Glacial Period.*—I have time to say but a word upon the field which is opened before us in this State for making calculations as to the date of the close of the glacial epoch. It is not well for the geologist to abandon his own chronological data for the confessedly uncertain speculations of astronomers upon this subject. Geologists have scarcely begun the systematic study of the evidences bearing upon the date of the glacial period. The evidences are three-fold: First, the amount of the glacial deposit; second, the extent of erosion since the glacial epoch; third, the extent to which glacial depressions have been filled with sediment.

The opportunities to estimate the extent of erosion since the glacial epoch are superabundant in Ohio. Each of the larger streams emptying into the Ohio River and into Lake Erie, and every tributary of those streams, presents a field by itself. In countless cases it is within our power to estimate with reasonable accuracy the number of cubic yards of material which the streams in the glaciated regions have removed from the till through which they flow. This would give us the *dividend*. It is by no means improbable that there are also many streams so nearly in their primitive condition that the rate of removal can be approximately estimated. This would give us the *divisor*. The *quotient* would give us the chronology of the close of the glacial period. The other hopeful field for chronological investigation in this State is presented in the numerous lakes which exist over the glaciated surface, and which, in most cases, owe their origin to the irregular deposition of till. It is not beyond hope that some of these may yield us the secret of their age. It may be possible to ascertain how deep a layer of sediment and peat has accumulated, and we may discover more specific facts concerning the rate of such accumulation. For a fuller discussion, see Chapter VI. in my "Studies in Science and Religion," Andover, W. F. Draper, 1882.

FOURTH. *Centers of Glacial Dispersion.*—Another topic to which we should give more attention relates to glacial movement, and to the centers from which the ice was dispersed. Ice, it should be remembered, behaves not like a solid but like a semi-fluid. If an oblong block of ice be suspended upon the ends it will gradually sag in the middle. If a strong hollow sphere be filled with water, and a good-sized orifice be left through which the ice may escape, and the whole be subjected to intense cold, the ice will project through the hole for a considerable distance. As a matter of fact, ice flows like cold molasses or half-hardened lava.

It is not necessary (as some might suppose) to have a steep declivity in order to secure glacial motion. Ice can move wherever water would run. In our conceptions of glacial movement we are in danger of having our ideas cramped by the contemplation of Alpine glaciers. The demands made upon our imagination by the glacial phenomena of North America are almost staggering to reason. We are called upon to believe that along a line thousands of miles in extent the ice-front of the great glacier rested upon land which is nowhere much lower—and in many places is actually higher—than the region from which it was dispersed. Boulders, in many cases, have been raised to a higher level than their native ledges.

Upon reflection, however, this is not so paradoxical as at a first glance it seems. It should be remembered that glacial ice is formed, not by the freezing of water upon lakes and oceans, but by the accumulation of snow, which, under its own pressure, becomes converted into ice. If, now, over an extensive level surface there should be precipitated annually six feet more of snow than melted, six thousand feet of ice would accumulate after a thousand years. It is thus easy to see that after a time the ice might form a mountain plateau by itself, and, owing to its semi-fluid character, it would gradually move away along whatever lines presented the least resistance. Such accumulations about the north pole would everywhere move to the south, and so we could get this southerly motion from the mere accumulation of ice about the pole, without supposing any change of level.

It is easy, also, to see that wherever—from climatic causes over any particular portion of this field—there should be an excessive accumulation of snow, that area would form a sub-center by itself, and project the ice-front in a loop south of the main line. The existence of such sub-centers I suppose to be, in part, the explanation of the various loops and irregular flexures which mark the glacial boundary in North America.

Nor is it difficult to conceive how boulders are raised in the ice to a higher than their original level. Indeed, I think I can conceive that fragments of rock can be picked up from beneath the glacier, and after movement over sufficient distance appear upon its surface; and I can easily believe that many of the well-known glaciated boulders scattered over the surface of Ohio have been repeatedly transferred from beneath the ice to its surface, and thence projected to the foot of the advancing ice-front, and afterwards re-elevated and projected again. This might be brought about as follows:

It is well known that the upper strata of glacial ice move faster than the lower, owing to the effect of friction in retarding the movement at the bottom. The result of this is that the upper side of the boulder which is imbedded in the ice is constantly subjected to a greater degree of onward pressure than the lower side. The effect of this must be to give an upward as well as an onward motion to the boulder in the ice. The course of such a boulder would be up a very gently inclined plane, the slower moving strata beneath it forming the incline, and the more rapidly moving upper strata being the force to push it along. Once upon the surface, if the motion were to continue long enough and the front were not too far away, the boulder might be transferred to the front and deposited before the moving mass; and if the glacier were still advancing, it would stand a chance to be covered again with ice, and to be re-incorporated in the moving mass to repeat another cycle.

CONCLUSION.

The glacial boundary line marked upon the map of Ohio is easily drawn when you know where to draw; but in reality it is about two hundred and fifty miles in length, and its determination could be secured only by exploring a belt about ten miles wide, and by travelling in the field a distance of more than one thousand miles. I have now zigzagged this line for the larger part of the distance from the end of Cape Cod to Illinois, and you will pardon me for entertaining some enthusiasm upon the subject,.and for having my imagination pretty well filled with the theme. The ice period of North America seems to me no longer a myth, but a reality. With my mind's eye I have seen it; I have walked along its front; I have beheld its glassy surface as it overlapped the mountain ranges of Pennsylvania, walled up its ancient river channels, filled up the depths of Lake Erie, and spread itself over the fairest fields of Ohio; and again I have seen it in its retreat, when its thickness was diminished, when its decaying southern border was obscured by the accumulations of materials which now form the moraine. I have seen it when the great streams of water from its melting surface had worn a series of parallel gorges in it along the line of the present water courses.   In imagination I have witnessed the enormous annual rise of the streams during the declining years of the glacial period.   I have seen the hardy palæolithic race who fished in these streams and hunted upon their banks, and were hastily driven from their homes by the rise of floods whose volume we can scarcely comprehend.   To the mental vision of him who goes over this field all these things become realities.   He has seen their signs: he has interpreted their handwriting.

I commend the study to the professional and business men who need to seek recreation and health in outdoor pursuits. Now that the buffalo is becoming scarce, and trout fishing unremunerative, we present to you for your vacation work the enticing sport of hunting for the terminal limits of the great American ice sheet, and for its imbedded marks of palæolithic man.

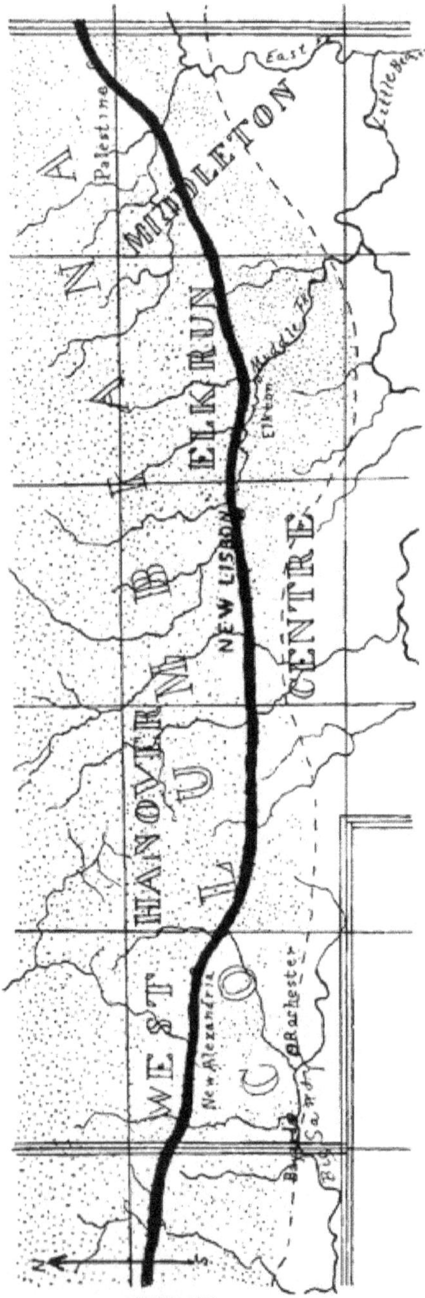

PLATE VIII.
Six miles to an inch.

PLATE IX.

DETAILED REPORT

OF

INVESTIGATIONS ALONG THE BOUNDARY

OF

The Glaciated Area in Ohio and Indiana,

CONDUCTED BY

PROF. G. FREDERICK WRIGHT, OF OBERLIN, OHIO,
IN THE SUMMER OF 1882.

COLUMBIANA COUNTY.

The boundary line of the glaciated region as it enters Ohio from Pennsylvania, is not so distinctly marked by large accumulations of till as in many other places ; so that it might create misapprehension to speak of a "terminal moraine" in Columbiana county. Still the boundary is well defined, and on penetrating the glaciated region a few miles, the accumulation of till is extensive. As we approached the Ohio line through the western counties of Pennsylvania, it was observed that what we have called "the fringe" became more extensive than in the eastern part of the State; that is, scattered granitic boulders and occasional accumulations of till are found in some places five or six miles south of the line bounding the continuous accumulation of till which envelops the larger part of the glaciated region. This peculiarity continues through Columbiana county, from east to west, and as far as Canton in Stark county.

For example: The accumulations of till worthy of being called a "terminal moraine," and of being reckoned as a continuation of that which marks the boundary of the glaciated region in New Jersey and Pennsylvania, enters Ohio at Palestine, Columbiana county, near the boundary of Unity and Middleton townships. The wagon road from Darlington to Palestine enters a great accumulation of till, near John Hartshorn's, about one-half mile south of the Pittsburgh, Ft. Wayne and Chicago R. R., and one mile east of Palestine. Here,

upon the land of the State Line Coal Works, upon a hill
sloping to the north, is a striking collection of granitic boulders, one of which measures 9x6x4 feet.   In the valley to the
north, through which the railroad runs, the accumulations of
drift show the modifying action of the glacial currents which
characterized the closing stages of the glacial period.   The
broken ridges and knobs of gravel, alternating with shallow
kettle-holes, remind one of the kames in New England.   Palestine is built upon such a formation.   A large granitic boulder
was here observed, in a freshly dug grave, five feet below the
surface.   A well was reported as penetrating till for fifty feet
without striking the bed rock.   Three-quarters of a mile
southwest from Palestine, a cut shows twenty feet of till ; but
boulders of granite and scratched stones with an occasional
slight deposit of till, were found several miles further south,
on the summits of the hills.   We walked from Smith's Ferry,
on the Ohio River, northward over the hills, to a point on
the State line east of Achor, in Middleton township, without finding any signs of glaciation.   Here granitic boulders
began to appear near Danison's coal bank.   On the summit
of the hill one-half mile west of Achor, and about 200 feet
higher than the bed of Little Beaver creek, is a granitic boulder
5x3x3 feet.   From this point northward to the moraine at
Palestine, these scattered but unmistakable evidences of the
presence of the glacier ice are found upon all the hill-tops.

After this description of the fringe, and its relation to the
moraine, we may pass more rapidly over the subject.   The
boundary of the fringe runs south-westward from Achor to
Clarkson post office, thence to the southeastern corner of Elk
Run township; thence westward along the southern line of
this township to the southeastern corner of Centre township;
thence it bears northerly, striking the line of Hanover township two miles northeast of Dungannon, thence westerly and
bearing a little south through Hanover township, passing one-
half mile south of Hanoverton Post Office, continuing west to
Bayard.   At Rochester there is an extensive kame-like deposit
filling the valley, which is here about one-half mile wide, in
which are numerous granitic pebbles from three to six inches

in diameter. One of these gravel ridges, running north by south, measured a little over 30 feet in height, with a slope of 20°. This cluster of kames is evidently due to the glacial floods pouring down the two branches of Big Sandy creek, which here unite. The accumulations of gravel in the valley of Big Sandy creek gradually diminish in amount and in coarseness from here on to Minerva, in Stark county. The ice all along here filled the valley and rose to the summit of the hills on the south. One boulder was found in the north-western corner of Augusta township, Carroll county, but an extensive *detour* of several miles to the south failed to discover any other signs of glaciation in that county. On returning to Bayard, till was found one-half mile southwest, rising upon the hills south of the valley to a height of 50 or 60 feet. One-half mile northwest of Bayard is a terrace 31 feet above the present flood-plain, enclosing a shallow, but extensive, kettle-hole between it and the hills to the north.

Retracing now our steps we find that from three to five miles north of the edge of this fringe there is a marked increase in the accumulation of till showing itself at East Palestine and near East Carmel Post Office. Thence across Elk Run township through Elkton to New Lisbon. The northeast part of Centre township is completely enveloped with till of an unknown depth. Three miles from New Lisbon and a quarter of a mile west, on the road to Teegarden, is a boulder of gneiss 8½x6½ feet, 4 feet out of ground. At and below New Lisbon, in the valley of the Middle Fork of Beaver, are the extensive accumulations of pebbles and coarse gravel which everywhere mark the streams as they issue from the line marking the terminal moraine. The terrace at New Lisbon shows no distinct stratification, and contains numerous pebbles from 10 to 15 inches in diameter, and at the railroad station is 36 feet above the river. Upon the north side, this extends for one mile down the stream. Still further down, similar terraces appear at intervals nearly to Elkton. The gravel in all these terraces is mined for kidney ore.

From New Lisbon west, the moraine runs through the northern part of Sections 23, 22, 21, 20 and 19 in Centre township.

In Hanover township it passes directly west, through the northern part of Sections 24, 23, 22, 21, 20 and 19. Two and a half miles northeast of Hanoverton, on the farm of Mr. Kinnely, the moraine is well developed, displaying its characteristic hummocks and kettle-holes upon the summit of the country. Large boulders are here very numerous, many from 3 to 5 feet in diameter. A mile or two farther north, near the state road, on the farm of Francis Blythe, is a granitic boulder 13x11 feet, 8 feet out of ground. Till is here certainly 16 feet deep, but how much more we could not ascertain.

Through West township the moraine bears slightly north, passing through the village of New Alexandria, which is situated upon a height of land, and surrounded by hummocks and kettle-holes of moderate size. Wells are reported 27 feet and 50 feet without striking rock. This continues through New Chambersburg, where wells were reported on the farm of Henry Bowers as going 27 feet without striking rock, the lower 6 feet in gravel an l sand.

STARK COUNTY.

The boundary line of the fringe in Stark county runs from Bayard northwest through Paris and Osnaburg townships, passing through the villages of Robertsville and Osnaburg. Boulders of large size are found a little back from this line in the eastern part of Paris township, some of them measuring between 7 and 8 feet. Two and a half miles southeast of Paris post office the last indications of ice-action are a few boulders in Section 15, one measuring 4x3x2 feet. West of Osnaburg the fringe becomes merged with the main accumulation.

The moraine proper passes through the northern sections of Paris and Osnaburg townships. One mile east of Paris post-office granitic boulders are numerous, and cuts in the till show it to be at least 10 feet deep upon the hills, and probably 20 feet. Three-quarters of a mile southwest of Paris, in the valley of Black Creek, the terrace of water-worn material is 15 feet above the stream, which is here small. The terraces are partially ridged, and contain shallow kettle-holes. On the farm of D. P. Sell, Section 6 of Paris township, wells are reported

30 feet deep, the first 8 feet being yellow till, the remaining 22 feet blue till. Another, 20 feet deep, ended in quicksand. This is on the high lands. Till completely envelops the southeastern corner of Nimishillin and the northeastern of Osnaburg townships. Kettle-holes are also apparent on the farm of H. Miller. In Section 2, Osnaburg township, on the farm of G. Hennigs, wells are reported 18, 20 and 26 feet, all in till. On a little higher land, in the southwest corner of Section 2, J. Anthony reported a well 14 feet through till. Till of unknown depth completely envelops the region for three miles south of Louisville post office. There are kame-like ridges in Section, 3 Osnaburg township, in a shallow valley along a branch of East Nimishillin Creek. The whole appearance of the country is as if filled up with till. Till continues on the road from Louisville to Osnaburg, where it suddenly ceases, at the corner of the diagonal road running to Robertsville. From Osnaburg southwest, for three miles, thence northwest three miles towards Canton, not a pebble or boulder was discovered. Much of the way the road is on high land, deep valleys opening southward-it being on the watershed between Nimishillin and Big Sandy. On crossing a small branch of the Nimishillin two and a half miles southeast of Canton, in the southwestern corner of Section 14 in Canton township, we struck suddenly into till on the north bank. From this point to Canton City till is continuous and granitic boulders are abundant. The depth of the till is unknown, but at various places cuts show it to be at least several feet deep. Sections 11 and 12, north of the Osnaburg road, are completely enveloped with till. A few rods northeast of the cemetery, about one mile east of Canton, are shallow kettle-holes in till. Upon the east branch of the Nimishillin the terrace facing the stream and a short distance back is 41 feet above the floood-plain. This contains many pebbles 16 inches and more in diameter. All are well rounded, and many are of local material. The cemetery, 20 rods farther east, is 16 feet higher, and is upon till. On the west side of the west branch of the Nimishillin the terrace rises in successive stages more than 80 feet, and its surface is very uneven. A mile and a half south of the city, below the junction of the two branches, there are

two well-marked terraces, the first of which is much the broader, and is 38 feet above the bed of the stream. The upper terrace, on the east side, is 36 feet higher, or 74 feet above the stream. The pebbles in the upper terrace were a mixture of granite and local rock, some of them a foot or more in diameter. One granitic pebble was more than 2 feet in diameter. The terrace on the west bank, near the Starr Mills, was by measurement 5 feet higher than that on the east.

A remarkable cluster of kame-like ridges covers the northwestern portion of Canton township and the northeastern of Perry, extending an unknown distance to the north. Meyer's Lake and Sippo Lake are enormous kettle-holes, and the whole region has much the appearance of Plymouth township in Massachusetts. Upon the south this kame-like belt is called Buck Ridge, and comes to a sudden termination near the crossing of the Fort Wayne and Chicago Railroad, two miles southwest of Canton City. Here an excellent section is made by the railroad. The kame rises 85 feet above the railroad, is coarsely stratified in places, contains many granitic pebbles (one of which measured 55x46x18 inches), and was 21½ feet higher than the railroad. There were large spaces in which no stratification appeared. There were pebbles upon the summit from 2 to 5 inches in diameter. The section exposed shows a base of 570 feet, with an altitude of 85 feet. The slope upon the east side varies from 18° to 25°; on the west side it is a little more gentle. (See cut in Geological Survey Ohio, vol. 2, p. 44.) An extensive sandy plain, full of gentle swells and ridges, stretches to the westward, while the space towards Canton is occupied by the more nearly level terrace. About 150 yards north of this section is a dry kettle-hole 25 feet deep, containing a granitic boulder 51x25x31 inches. Another dry kettle-hole near by is about 300 feet long, 200 feet wide, and 40 feet deep, with sides sloping inward 24°. The rims of these kettle-holes are at the summit of the kame.

From my experience elsewhere, I should expect to be able to trace a series of kames northward from this point, and find it enclosing the lakes in the southern part of Summit county, and particularly abundant south of Akron.

From Canton westward the fringe pretty much disappears, and the moraine bears rapidly southward, running across the southeastern corner of Perry township, and continuing in a south-southwestern course to the southern part of Bethlehem township, crossing the Tuscarawas River about two miles above Bolivar; thence it bears more westward, crossing the southeastern portion of Sugar Creek township, and the northwestern corner of Wayne township in Tuscarawas county, entering Holmes county east of Weinsburg.

It is difficult to exaggerate the sharpness of this portion of the boundary line. Retracing our course, our notes show that the line bounding the till passes through the middle of Section 29 Canton township, where it crosses a small stream running to the north. This, like many other similar cases, showed signs of having been dammed up, thus producing a small temporary glacial lake. To the north and west the till is continuous, and probably of great depth; to the east it suddenly disappears, half way up a low hill. From Richville to the southeastern corner of Perry township till and boulders are continuous, and the deposit apparently of great depth. One of the boulders a short distance beyond the till measured 6x4½ feet. A detour through Section 6, Pike township, and Section 32, Canton township, demonstrated a total absence of glacial signs in that region. The whole country to the southeast was broken and hilly, in striking contrast to that in the opposite direction, which seems to have been leveled up by glacial material. Upon the hills in Section 1, Bethlehem township, cuts in the till 6 feet in depth disclose large granitic boulders lying still deeper. The road running south, between Sections 11 and 12, and 13 and 14, is upon the very edge of the glaciated region. Detours of a few rods to the east lead into a region in which there is only rock in place and the soil formed by its disintegration. Southwestward from this point to the river, the boundary is near an unfrequented road passing one-half mile north of the first Moravian settlement in this region.

At the upper end of the great ox-bow in the Tuscarawas River upon which Bolivar is built, but on the north side of the river, is an immense kame-like accumulation, containing boulders from 2½ to 3 feet in diameter. The terrace is here 36 feet above the river, and the kame-like áccumulation is 118 feet higher. The space included in the ox-bow is occupied by a gravel deposit whose surface is 51 feet above the river. From this point down, the river occupies a narrower valley, with diminishing terraces. Five miles below, at Zoar, wells in this terrace 30 feet deep do not go through the gravel. Above the ox-bow, and on the west side of the river—opposite the kame-like deposit just described —the terrace is 61 feet, which continues up the river a mile or more without change.

Going west along a road near the county line in Bethlehem, a little till appeared when the higher land was reached, but on ascending the hills to the left (south) it disappeared, and is wholly absent in the extreme southwestern corner of Bethlehem township. But the hills in Section 30, immediately to the north, are covered with till containing large granitic boulders, some of which are between 3 and 4 feet in diameter. Till is continuous, and of unknown depth, all the rest of the way to Navarre, displaying to some extent the familiar kettle-holes and knolls of the moraine belt. The small streams emptying north also display the well-known signs of temporary ice-dams. One of the numerous boulders of red granite over this area was between 200 and 300 feet above the Tuscarawas River, and measured 7x5 feet, 3 feet out of ground.

The characteristics of the moraine just described continue through the southern portion of Sugar Creek township, crossing Sugar Creek below Beech City. One and a half miles below Beech City, towards Deardoff's Mills, the accumulations of gravel in the valley are immense. The valley is here about one mile wide. The gravel is thrown up into hummocks and ridges from 20 to 30 feet above the general level, enclosing many kettle-holes. The country from this point to Wilmot, and from Wilmot south to the county line, is completely enveloped in till. One boulder measured 7x6 feet, 2½ feet out of ground. But on the road from Deardoff's Mills, across the northern part of Wayne township in Tuscarawas county, toward Weinsburg in Holmes county, no till or boulders appeared for several miles. The road leads over the summit of the land, and displays, to good effect on either side, the contrasts between the glaciated and unglaciated region. One mile and a half east of the Holmes county line granitic boulders begin to appear, and accompanied after a little with till, continue to increase to Weinsburg. This east and west road enters the moraine at an acute angle, the direction of the moraine being here west-southwest. The northeast portion of Paint township, in Holmes county, is covered with till to an unknown, but evidently to a great depth.

HOLMES COUNTY.

The glacial boundary in Holmes county is very sharply defined, dividing the county into two nearly equal portions. It enters the county on the east, in Paint township, near the corner of Stark and Tuscarawas counties, and passes diagonally to the northeast corner of Berlin township, where it turns more nearly west, passing through Hardy township, crossing the Killbuck below Millersburg; thence, bearing slightly to the north, it passes through the centre of Monroe and the northern part of Knox township, to the eastern side of Hanover township in Ashland county. Through all this distance the contrasts between the regions north and south of this line are very marked.

In Paint township there is but little till south of the diagonal road leading from Wilmot through Weinsburg to Berlin. Driving one-quarter of a mile south of Weinsburg, till suddenly disappears. There is a noteworthy collection of granitic boulders a few rods southeast of the village, at the crossing of the road from Slatersville. South of this there is no till. Occasional boulders were reported, but none were seen by us in a drive of half a mile. To the north and east of Weinsburg the deposit of till is continuous, and evidently of great depth. Weinsburg is on the watershed between Sugar Creek and Indian Trail Creek, and according to our barometer was 600 feet above the valley of the Killbuck at Millersburg. The southwestern part of Paint and the southeastern of Salt Creek townships are likewise covered with till, which is evidently very deep. A granitic boulder on the road between Weinsburg and Mount Hope measured 7x6 feet, 3 feet out of ground.

BERLIN TOWNSHIP.

A detour of several miles through the southern portion of this township disclosed no sign of glaciation, except in the valley of Dowdy Creek. In this valley there are extensive terraces down as far as within one mile of the southern boundary. At that point the terrace is 50 feet above the stream and about 150 yards wide, and contains some scratched pebbles. The boundary of the till runs between Sections 13 and 8, and crosses the western boundary of the township one-half mile south of the road running between Berlin and Millersburg. The elevation here is 475 feet (B) above the Killbuck. Granitic boulders are abundant all along this road. At Berlin post office it is 600 feet (B). On driving north from Berlin post office we strike immediately into till, which seems to be very deep. Near the corner of the road turning east one-quarter of a mile north, in Section 6, are extensive kame-like accumulations containing numerous boulders, and enclosing a large kettle-hole. Till is continuous northward.

HARDY TOWNSHIP.

On the road from Millersburg to Berlin till is found on the tops of the hills all along to the township line. Going east from Millersburg the first hill is 250 feet above the railroad, the second 350 feet, thence rising at the town line to 475 feet. The depth of the till is at least several feet. In Section 14 a boulder measured 7x5 feet, 3 feet out of ground. The most southerly deposit of till on the east side of the Killbuck is where the north branch of Sandy Run touches Section 16, two miles and a half southeast of Millersburg. Three-quarters of a mile northeast of this point a small accumulation of till and boulders occur, at a height of 375 feet above the run; east and south the country is entirely free from it.

The terraces upon the Killbuck are extensive, both above and below the glacial limit. One mile and a half below Millersburg on the west side, on the farm of A. Uhl, is a terrace about a quarter of a mile wide, containing kame-like ridges and knolls, the surface of which is 102 feet above the floodplain. This gradually rises until it is merged in the till of

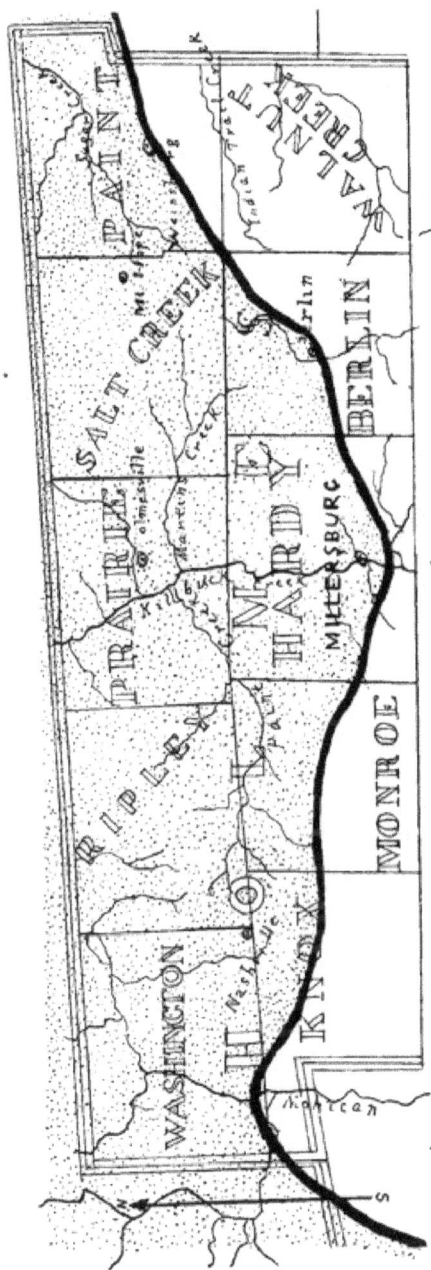

PLATE X.

PLATE XI.

the hills beyond. Two miles further south, in the northwest corner of Mechanic township, near Stuart's Mills, the terrace is composed of finer material, and is level topped and gradually descends towards the south, being here but 71 feet above the flood-plain. Still further below the glacial limit at Oxford is a terrace on the east side of the creek, extending across the open ends of the ox-bow which the stream here forms. The intervale is here about one-third of a mile wide, and 25 feet above low-water mark. The terrace is 76 feet higher. On the west side of the creek, between Shimplin's Run and Black Creek, and one-quarter mile west of the Killbuck, are terraces of fine material containing some granitic gravel, which are 61 feet above the flood-plain.

Driving up from Millersburg, on the west side of the Killbuck, there are no terraces for the first mile. The valley is about one-half mile wide. But just above where a small stream comes in from the west is a kame-like accumulation of coarse material, 50 feet in height, extending about one-eighth of a mile. On the north side of this small stream the material is finer, and the surface much more uneven, extending to the road running over the hills to Holmesville.

Near Holmesville—five miles above Millersburg—Paint, Killbuck, and Martin's Creek come together nearly at right angles. About their junction there is an extensive intervale not far from two miles in diameter. The village is built upon a terrace about 25 feet above the intervale. Between the Killbuck and Martin's Creek, which comes in from the east, there is a kame-like accumulation of rather fine material (the pebbles being ordinarily not more than three inches in diameter) extending about one-eighth of a mile N. W. by S. E. The surface is very much broken, displaying many kettle-holes. A railroad cutting through it shows some scratched stones in the material, and a depth of 61 feet at the railroad; but it rises about 40 feet higher to the north. From this point to Millersburg, on the east side, there are no terraces, the intervale being about one-sixth of a mile wide. One-half a mile north of Millersburg, as the road rises over the hill, a fresh cut in the till of 20 feet disclosed no bottom to it.

On the west side of the Killbuck, in Hardy township, till ceases, two miles and a-half southwest of Millersburg, on the farm of William Lisle. There is here a small stream, and the till appears upon the north side of the stream, but not upon the south. The general elevation of the country (which is much broken) is 350 feet above the Killbuck. Southeast, for two miles, till is totally absent, while to the north it is abundant, and boulders are numerous. It continues west to the works of the Hardy Coal Company, from which place to Oxford no till appears.

MONROE TOWNSHIP.

From Oxford we drove in a northwest direction up a small stream which rises in the centre of Monroe township. No boulders or till appeared below Centreville ; but there were terraces of fine material containing some granitic pebbles, and diminishing in height as we ascended the stream. North from Centreville granitic boulders began to appear, and were frequent all along up the valley to the watershed, where, near W. S. Carn's, a large deposit of till appeared, enveloping everything and forming large dome-shaped hills. Cuts from 10 to 15 feet disclose no rocks. The road is 300 feet (B) above the Killbuck, but hills covered with till are about 150 feet higher.

Oak Grove Nursery, a short distance to the west, is 475 (B) above the Killbuck. One-quarter of a mile farther west, on lower ground, the deposit of till and boulders is very marked: one of granite measured 10½x6½ feet, 3½ feet out of the ground. Elevation 430 feet (B). Till is continuous one mile west, and south to the farm of R. Martin. For the next mile and a half there were occasional boulders, but no till. On the next road west, struck suddenly into till by a school-house, whose elevation is 610 (B) above the Killbuck. Beyond this there were occasional boulders to the road near the western line of the township, leading to Napoleon. Some boulders were seen half a mile farther south. This is about five miles northeast of Napoleon, which is situated in the valley of Black Creek, which is about one-eighth of a mile wide, and

from 400 feet to 500 feet below the general level.   A striking
feature along this creek, and especially in the vicinity of
Napoleon, is the great blocks of sandstone, formerly occupying the summits of the hills, which have been broken off, and
have gradually crept down towards the bottom as the underlying shale and talus have been removed. These blocks are
sometimes as large as a house, and are in all stages of advancement in their progress towards the valley. They resem-
ble in most respects what is to be seen in the valley of the
Alleghany south of Salamanca, and in the neighborhood of
Rock City. Instead of being due, as some have supposed, to
glacial action, these phenomena are pretty certain evidence of
the absence of any glacial movement, and exist either alto-
gether south of the line of glaciation, or, as here and at Rock
City, on the very margin, where the ice-movement ceased,
and where glacial abrasion was reduced to zero.

KNOX TOWNSHIP.

From Napoleon we followed up the narrow valley of Black
Creek on the road to Nashville. The valley continues to be
about one-eighth of a mile wide, and for five miles is remarkable both for the abundance of the sandstone blocks referred
to above, which are creeping down the sides, and for the
absence of granitic boulders. Upon reaching the farm of
A. Cline, a little south of the watershed, till appeared in
great quantities. This is 375 feet (B) above Napoleon. From
here to Nashville till is continuous for 2½ miles, as also southwest of Nashville to the hill south of the farm of S. H. Vance.
Boulders continued to the cross-roads south of the house of
A. Bell, where all signs of glaciation had ceased. West of
this there are no signs of glaciation as far as the next cross-
roads. Elevation 450 feet (B) above Napoleon. Turning
north, one mile brought us into a kame-like deposit in a shallow valley by the cross-road, near G. Uhlman's, one mile
south of Washington township, and three miles east of Hanover township in Ashland county. This kame is about 25
feet high, and its course is nearly parallel with that of the
shallow valley in which it is situated, which drains into the
Mohican. What is marked near here, on the county atlas, as

an ancient mound is more ancient than the map-maker supposed, it being not artificial, but a small mound of slate left by erosion. From here northwest, to a point a little above the junction of Lake Fork with Mohican River, till and boulders are continuous. This is near the southwest corner (Section 12) of Washington township. From this point down to the junction and a half mile beyond, is a terrace of very coarse material, largely composed of granitic pebbles. Elevation above the river 107 feet. No till was discovered in the western projection of Knox township. From this point we drove through Nashville to Millersburg, on a road parallel with the glacial boundary, and about two miles north of it. Till is continuous, and evidently deep, there being but few out-cropping rocks in the whole distance. Cuts in the till frequently showed a depth of from 10 to 15 feet, with no signs of bottom. Two wells were reported, on the hills crossed, as going 25 feet without striking rock. Boulders are everywhere abundant. To the north stretches the characteristic levelled area of the glaciated region. The ice, with its burdens, evidently came up to the watershed between Paint Creek and Black Creek—its serrated edge barely surmounting it.

KNOX COUNTY.

The boundary line of the glaciated region, which, in the western part of Holmes county, was bearing slightly northward, suddenly turns to the south in the eastern part of Hanover township, Ashland county; passing thence into Jefferson, the northeastern township of Knox county, and thence through the western portions of Union, Butler, and Jackson townships, along the eastern margin of the county. The change of direction was so abrupt as at first to confuse, and afterwards to startle us. But, as usual, we found the departure from the general law of glacial movement less than would at first seem to be the case. From Salamanca, in New York, the moraine, with slight variations, bears continually southward, as well as westward.

JEFFERSON TOWNSHIP.

There are a few granitic boulders, and some glacial gravel, on the road from Jelloway to Greersville, one-half mile east of Greersville. Near the same place on the Danville road, by the Methodist church, there is a larger collection of pebbles, and perhaps till. This is in a valley, on a branch of the Jelloway, running south. But the hill to the west is free from drift ; likewise the hill to the east, occupying Sections 4 and 7, is without till. But in the valley of a small tributary to the Mohican, a little south and east, in Sections 3 and 8, there are accumulations of till in ridges from 10 to 15 feet high. These are best shown upon the farm of G. Greer, in Section 8. From this point to the south line of the township till is continuous, but does not extend eastward into Sections 12 and 19. The Cleveland, Akron, and Delaware Railroad enters the glaciated region from the east through a cut in till, one mile east of Danville, and very nearly upon the line between Jefferson and Union townships. This cut is 375 paces long, and is from 20 to 36 feet in depth. The pebbles average from 2 to 3 inches ; but there are a few boulders of considerable size. The hills to the southeast show no till.

UNION TOWNSHIP.

The old village of Danville is built upon a hill in the extreme northwestern part of the township. The height of this hill is by barometer exactly the same as that of the depot at Mount Vernon. This hill is composed of till. A. J. Workman reports a well 126 feet deep as passing through yellow clay, blue clay, gravel, quick-sand, and cemented gravel, and still not reaching rock. Another well of 65 feet, through similar material, was reported. One and a half mile south of Danville, on the Millwood road, a large deposit of till forms the divide between Owl Creek and Mohican River. The east and west line of this deposit is sharply defined, running through the eastern part of Section 14, and the central part of Section 17, to Millwood. On the east side of the small brook, running into Millwood from the north, drift is absent ; but on the west side it is bounded by a range of gravelly knolls and kame-like ridges. These are composed of glacial material, and are 117 feet above the brook on the north of the village.

BUTLER TOWNSHIP.

On the south side of Owl Creek a thin deposit of till covers the whole western range in Butler township, the boundary line swinging a little to the east until it enters Jackson township in the northeastern corner of Section 4. But the deposit is nowhere so marked in this township as to deserve to be called a "terminal moraine." The limit, however, is pretty sharply defined.

JACKSON TOWNSHIP.

In this township the boundary line enters upon the north, two miles east from Clay township, and continues in a southeasterly direction to the south line, about three miles east of Clay township. At the cross roads in Section 8, we turned east into till of considerable evident depth. This disappeared in three-fourths of a mile, and did not reappear until we had gone one mile south to the church in Section 12, and turned west one-half mile. Here, on turning the summit of the hill, two miles north from the south, and $2\frac{1}{4}$ miles east of the west line, we struck into a continuous deposit of till stretching westward. This is upon the watershed, and is 300 feet (B) above Wakatomaka Creek. Upon crossing this creek, and striking the Zanesville road in the northeast corner of Eden township, Licking county, and driving northwest to Martinsburg, found till of great depth all the way. Occasionally the tops of the hills exposed rock in place, but Paul Run is nearly filled with till.

LICKING COUNTY.

The glacial boundary line enters Licking county in the northeast corner of Eden township, passes through the northwest corner of Mary Ann, the eastern sides of Newark and Licking townships, nearly on the line between the latter and Franklin and Bowling Green townships.

EDEN TOWNSHIP.

From Fallsburgh Post Office to Simpkin's corner, in the extreme northwestern portion of the township, the road follows the watershed. No till or boulders whatever appear upon it. At Simpkin's corner a few granitic pebbles appear, but there is no till until reaching the farm of A. D. Larrason, in Eden township, one-eighth of a mile south of the Knox county line, and three-quarters of a mile west from the line between Fallsburgh and Eden township. This is upon a height of land about 350 feet above the creek, and granitic boulders three and four feet in diameter are abundant. Patches of till continued to appear upon the road following the watershed south for 2½ miles; crossed Rocky Fork near J. Elliott's ; there was but little drift in this valley at this point. Upon ascending the watershed to the west, in Section 13, found a considerable depth of till, which continued for a half mile west and a quarter of a mile south ; but the diagonal road running southeast, and keeping along the watershed between Rocky Fork and Wilkin's Run shows no till to the town line ; but a few white granitic boulders were observed. Till, however, appeared 1½ miles west in the valley of Wilkin's Run.

MARY ANN TOWNSHIP.

The deposit of till is not continuous over the western part of Mary Ann, but a considerable amount appears in Section 6, and the southwestern corner of the township is completely enveloped in a deep deposit.

The terrace deposits in the neighborhood of Wilkin's Run post office are noteworthy. One-half mile southwest of the post office this terrace is 92 feet high, and composed of water-worn pebbles with no large boulders. This continues up the small branch nearly to the line of Madison township, where it merges into the deposit of till. Two miles east of Wilkin's Run the deposit is still noteworthy, and presents the appearance of extensive kames. The southwest corner of this township, and the southeast of Newton, are deeply enveloped in till. Wilkin's Run was one of the glacial outlets, and the terrace deposits are such as usually mark the streams as they emerge from the boundary of the glaciated region.

At the city of Newark the three forks of the Licking River unite. All of these drain the glaciated region upon whose eastern border Newark is situated. The extensive gravel plain upon which the city is built is about 20 feet above the river, and is the deposit of these streams in the last stages of the glacial period when still swollen by the floods of the melting glacier; while terraces of a still higher altitude surround the plain, marking the size of the floods at a somewhat earlier date, when at their greatest extent. The terrace upon which the city cemetery is situated is 108 feet above Licking River. Southeast of the city, a terrace near the river is something over 60 feet above it. The eastern limit of till in this township coincides in the northern part with the east line of the township, though in this part of the township many of the hills are free from till. As, however, you go east from the North Fork, along the town-line road, between Newark and Newton, the till appears to be of great depth, and stretches away to the north in such hummocks and ridges as usually characterize the moraine. The elevation here is 200 feet (B) above the North Fork. South of the city, on the Linnville road, till envelops everything to the summit of the high lands, where it is evidently of great depth. The elevation is about 300 (B) above Newark.

The glacial boundary follows very closely the line between Licking and Franklin townships. To the west everything is enveloped in till; to the east are the familiar rocks and gorges of the unglaciated region. Many boulders were found, and a considerable amount of drift, along Claylick Creek, in the centre of Franklin township. This, however, seems to be a water deposit, formed by streams and floating ice, which came over the low place between Swamp Run and Claylick Creek. The gap in the watershed between these streams is

150 feet lower than that of the hills to the north and south, and the valley through which Claylick Creek now empties to the north appears to be very narrow. There certainly is no till on the hills, either to the northwest or southeast of this depression. The road along the town line, from Hog Run to Amsterdam, in the southwest corner of Franklin, is all the way over a deep deposit of till containing many granitic boulders. Amsterdam is 400 feet (B) above Newark, and commands a most extensive view of the fertile and level glaciated region to the west, and of the broken region to the east. Near the Presbyterian Church upon the most commanding point near Amsterdam, is an Indian mound 21 feet high, and 124 paces in circumference. East of Amsterdam a drive of three miles to Linnville disclosed no till, but south and west the deposit is continuous and deep. In the southeastern part of Licking township, east of the reservoir, the road runs for half a mile upon the summit of a ridge of kame-like hills containing many granitic boulders. This ridge seems to cross the valley, and to be a true moraine barrier, restraining the waters of Reservoir Lake. The railroad near here shows very good sections of this ridge, and of other ridges parallel to it. They are from 15 to 30 feet above the level of the valley, but how much of their base is obscured by subsequent deposits there is no means of telling. Through this depression east of the reservoir, on the line between Licking and Perry counties, there was evidently a great overflow of glacial water, emptying through Jonathan Creek into the Muskingum, below Zanesville.

PERRY COUNTY.

The moraine passes in this county, in a north and south direction, through Thorn and Reading townships.

THORN TOWNSHIP.

We have already described the glacial accumulations east of the reservoir, where they pass from Licking county into this township. The reservoir occupies a great kettle-hole. The railroad which here cuts through the moraine follows for several miles towards the southeast an outlet for the glacial floods. This occupies a valley about a mile wide, through the middle of which kame-like ridges of gravel 15 to 20 feet in height extend ; but these are flanked on either side by deposits of black muck. On turning up a tributary towards Somerset, these deposits cease. The headwaters of the stream are in an unglaciated region.

Thornville is upon a hill of till containing numerous granitic boulders, and which is about 300 feet (B) above Newark. A well upon this hill was reported as passing through 10 feet of soil, 25 feet of blue clay. Southeast from Thornville the till is, for the first mile, very deep, with very numerous and large granitic boulders. Till continues a mile farther to Section 23, and thence south to the northwest corner of Reading township. But from Section 23, Thorn township, to Somerset (seven miles southeast), and thence west to the branch of Rush Creek, a mile west of New Reading, the country is wholly unglaciated.

READING TOWNSHIP.

The northwestern section of Reading township presents a level and rich expanse of territory, produced by the glacial floods coming down from the southern part of Thorn township. The contrast between the western sections of this township and everything east of Rush Creek is very marked. The road running south, near the western line of this township, is through a region deeply enveloped in till, as far as the pike, a little east of Rushville. A drive on the pike, of half a mile, into Reading township, toward Somerset, brings one into the unglaciated region.

FAIRFIELD COUNTY.

The glacial boundary enters Fairfield county, a little south of the Somerset and Lancaster pike in Richland township, and crosses the northwest corner of Rush Creek township, the southeast corner of Pleasant township, the northwest corner of Bern, through the center of Hocking township, and the western sections of Madison township to the line between Pickaway and Hocking counties.

RICHLAND TOWNSHIP.

The Somerset and Lancaster pike suddenly enters extensive deposits of till, upon passing from Perry to Fairfield county, a mile and a half east of East Rushville; but a drive of a half mile south carries one entirely beyond the range of till. From Rushville one must drive a mile and a half south to reach the unglaciated district. But here on both sides of the creek, the passage from the glaciated to the unglaciated is sudden. On the north part of H. Geiger's farm, east of Rush Creek, and one-half mile north of the township line, the glacial limit is marked by hummocks of till, which are at least 50 feet in depth; while on the west side of the creek the boundary is near the town line in Rush Creek township, on the farm of J. D. Martin. Large granitic boulders abound along the glaciated margin through Richland township. The elevation is 250 feet (B) above Lancaster, and about 200 feet above Rush Creek. There is no barrier in this vicinity to stop the southern progress of the ice. A detour of several miles to Bremen demonstrated the absence of till to the southeast.

RUSH CREEK TOWNSHIP.

The characteristics of the glacial boundary through Rush Creek township are very similar to those in Richland. The remnants of a boulder of dark, hornblendic rock, on the farm of J. D. Martin, one-fourth south of West Rushville, measured 10x8x3 feet out of ground. Probably one-third had been removed by blasting. The elevation is 250 feet above Lancaster, and there is no southern barrier to account for the sudden termination of the till. Four or five miles to the south, across the valley of the west branch of Rock Creek, an escarpment of Waverly sandstone hills is a striking feature of the landscape. There is no till in Sections 17 and 18 of this township.

PLEASANT TOWNSHIP.

From Rushville to Lancaster the pike bears southwest. The glacial boundary enters Pleasant township, one mile south of the pike, intersecting the pike again near where it passes from Pleasant township to Bern. The road running to Lancaster,

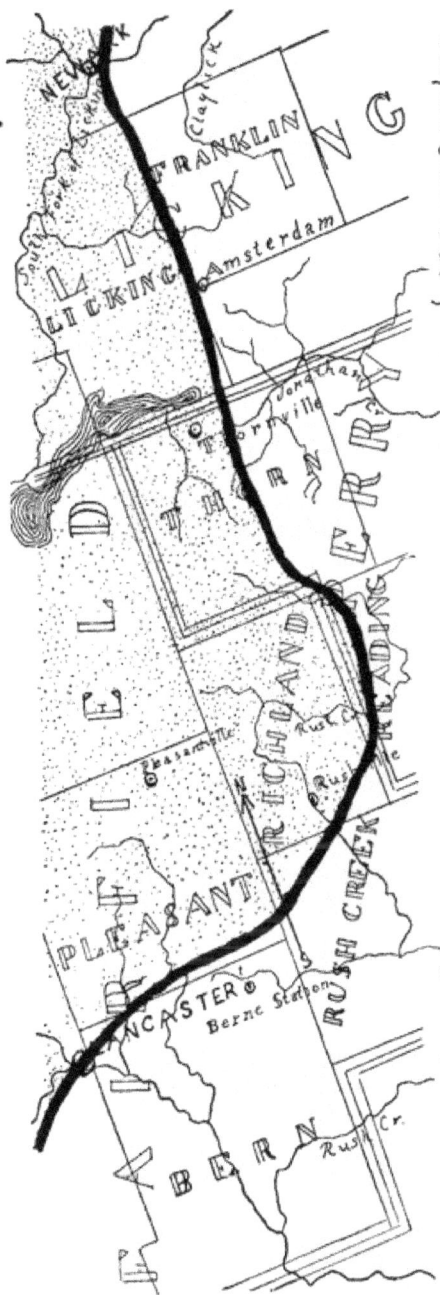

PLATE XII.

PLATE XIII.

parallel with the pike, and about one mile northwest, is through a region everywhere enveloped with till, a great amount of it resting upon the hills 250 feet above the city. It is at the intersection of this road with that to Pleasantville that the celebrated granitic boulder referred to by Professor Andrews (see his Geology, pp. 211, 212) is found. This is in the valley of Baldwin's Run, is hornblendic in character, and measures 18x12x6 feet out of ground. Boulders were left upon the summit of Pleasant Mountain, a mile north of Lancaster, and about 300 feet above it.

BERN TOWNSHIP.

The moraine enters the northwest corner of Bern township, near the city of Lancaster, but its course is here somewhat disguised by the water action in the Hocking Valley, which it here intersects. The Cincinnati and Muskingum Valley Railroad, east of Lancaster, passes through a low valley into the tributaries of Rush Creek. This valley is bounded upon the south by an escarpment of Waverly sandstone, rising about 250 feet. A drive across the country, back of this escarpment, from Lancaster to Bern Station, failed to disclose any signs of glaciation ; but the valley itself is partially filled with gravel, brought in by the various glacial tributaries from the north. This deposit of gravel is especially noticeable near Bern Station, where the gravel accumulation brought down by Raccoon Creek, forms a hill 50 or 60 feet in height. Till and boulders appear between the Logan and Chillicothe road, at an elevation of about 50 feet, one mile south of Lancaster.

HOCKING TOWNSHIP.

The course of the Mayesville and Zanesville turnpike, through Hocking township, is everywhere over a vast deposit of till. This is true not only when it follows up the valley of Hunter's Run, parallel with and close to the railroad, but after it crosses the railroad to the south, and rises upon hills which are 450 feet above Lancaster, near the southwest corner of the town. Here the till is piled up to a great height, upon the summit of the sandstone escarpment which overlooks the plains to the north made smooth and fertile by glacial action. On the farm of S. Peters, in Section 20, 450 feet above the canal at Lancaster, a well was reported 40 feet in till ; another, near by, 20 feet. The parallel road, two miles southeast, shows no till from Hamburg post office toward Lancaster,for three miles, to its intersection with Arney's Run; for the rest of the distance till is continuous and deep. But occasional granitic boulders crown the summit of the sandstone hills running parallel with these roads and half-way between them, and rising 450 feet above the canal. Muddy Prairie, in the south-western corner of this township, is a shallow kettle-hole of great size, which has been filled by the accumulation of peat. Its natural drainage is by a long circuit to the west, but by a little ditching it is made to empty by a shorter course through Muddy Prairie Run.

MADISON TOWNSHIP.

On leaving Lancaster the glacial boundary turns rapidly toward the south, and passes through Madison township nearly in a north and south direction, through Sections 4, 9, 16, and 21. It crosses Clear Creek at Clearport, near the junction with Muddy Run, at an elevation of about 200 feet (B) above Lancaster. Everywhere along this distance the glacial accumulation abuts closely against an escarpment of Waverly sand-stone ; yet covers hills to the west, in Clear Creek township, of equal height with them, namely, 450 feet above Lancaster. The line bends a little west as it emerges from this township, and enters Hocking county.

PICKAWAY AND HOCKING COUNTIES

The moraine follows so nearly the line between Pickaway and Hocking counties that we shall do best to consider them together.

Driving east from Tarleton, in Pickaway, to the line of Hocking,till and granitic boulders are continuous and abundant to the Hocking line, and for nearly a mile farther east ; but here they suddenly cease, and do not reappear on turning north until reaching Section 20, in Madison township, Fair-field county. Driving southeast from Tarleton, till is continu-ous until crossing the county line, northwest of South Perry

post office. A section of till upon the county line here shows
at least 30 feet in depth. The elevation is 300 feet above
Circleville. One mile east of the county line till had entirely
disappeared. There is no till in the valley of Laurel Run for
a mile and a half west of South Perry. Hills of Waverly sandstone arise on every side about the village. There is no till
upon them, but a granitic fragment 6 in. by 4 in. was found
upon a hill a few rods north of the village, and 225 feet (B)
above it. This is 300 feet above Circleville. Across the Run,
on the south side, the ridge road to Adelphi rises 375 feet in
one and one-half miles, and turns west upon the summit,
near the southern line of Perry township, and three miles
from its western boundary. This is by barometer 450 feet
above Circleville, and the level touches the tops of the hills
in all directions. This road continues for three miles west
upon the summit of a narrow ridge of sandstone, left by the
erosion of the streams. From it one looks down on either
side into gorges between 300 and 400 feet in depth. On driving
upon this ridge about three miles westward, we struck a collection of granitic pebbles upon the very summit, about one
mile northeast of the southwest corner of the township. The
pebbles were small, but of a variety of kinds. Three-fourths
of a mile farther west, while still 275 feet above South Perry,
began to find till. Granitic boulders continue frequent to
Laurelville, at the junction of Salt Creek and Laurel Creek.
The level of the stream is here 75 feet lower than that at
South Perry.

ROSS COUNTY.

Nowhere in Ohio is the glacial boundary marked by larger
accumulations than in Ross County, through which it extends
diagonally from the northeast corner to the southwest—passing
through the northwest corner of Colerain, the southern part
of Green, the southern part of Union, the northern edge of
Twin, the southeastern part of Paint, and the western part of
Paxton townships.

COLERAIN TOWNSHIP.

The village of Adelphi occupies the northeast section of
Colerain township, and is built upon an irregular deposit of

till worthy to be compared with the terminal moraine on Cape
Cod in Massachusetts, and with that upon the Pocono plateau
in Pennsylvania, and that west of Canton in Stark county.
Salt Creek bursts through this moraine a few rods northeast
of the corner of the county, and makes off to the southeast,
through a narrow valley 450 feet deep, and for a short distance is bounded on the east by extensive gravel terraces.
The moraine accumulation upon which Adelphi is built abuts
upon this creek towards the east, and there is here a perpen-
dicular exposure of till 188 feet in depth. The creek is constantly undermining it, and an extensive slide is in progress
which has already carried away a considerable portion of the
cemetery. The height of this cemetery was taken by level.
West of the village where the land is higher the barometer
indicated more than 200 feet. On driving south from Adelphi, up Brimstone Hollow, till continued for one mile, and
occasional granitic pebbles were found for two miles farther,
where the summit of the Waverly sandstone escarpment was
reached, at a height of 400 feet (B) above Salt Creek. Turning west upon this ridge, a little till was found upon the very
summit after going a mile, and just before beginning to
descend towards the north into the valley of Reed's Ford.
On descending into this valley, a hundred feet or more, drift
began to appear. This was at first water-worn, and in terraces,
as would be natural in a valley beginning, as this does, a little
south of the glaciated line, and opening to the north. On
reaching Section 14, near the residence of Isaac Delong, till
appeared in large quantities, with many granitic boulders,
some of them from 6 to 8 feet in diameter. On going a mile
and a half farther north, this road reaches the turnpike, two
miles from Adelphi, which, over all this distance, follows the
summit of a true moraine deposit. To the northwest, stretch
the fertile plains of Pickaway county, lying fully 150 feet
lower than the summit of this moraine. To the south rises,
near by, the escarpment of Waverly sandstone, which forms
the northwestern boundary of the great coal formations of
the State. The granitic pebbles which we had found upon the
summit of that escarpment in Ross, in Hocking, and in Fair-

field counties, show that the ice was at least 400 feet thick over all the plains to the north.

This moraine ridge continues southwest from Adelphi in about the same proportions, and in similar relations, to the plain upon the north, and to the hills upon the south, until it enters Green township, two miles from the southern border. All along through Colerain township, in driving a mile south from the pike, one strikes out of the till, and after crossing a little valley, plunges into the deep gorges which everywhere characterize the sandstone regions beyond. Professor Orton had noted the boundary with great accuracy. (See Ohio's Geol. Report, Vol. II, pp. 651, 652.)

GREEN TOWNSHIP.

The moraine enters Green township from the east in Section 24. Till continued to the northern edge of Section 25, where it suddenly disappeared on the watershed. A drive of two miles south into Harrison township demonstrates the total absence of till over the southeast corner of Green. On driving over the diagonal road northwest till appeared at the watershed in Section 25, nearly one mile from the south line, and a mile and a half from the east line of Green township. The accumulation of till is large along the road between Sections 26 and 27. The diagonal road running southwest through Sections 27 seems directly upon the moraine, and between this glacial accumulation and the rocky hills to the south there is a space of about half a mile, occupied by a small stream whose headwaters are in Section 33. In the southern part of Section 29 there are enormous kame-like ridges of gravel, from 100 to 150 feet (B) in height, and running north and south. The material of this kame is rather fine, and is largely composed of limestone pebbles. The Pickaway plains here contract into the valley of the Scioto, which, through the rest of its course, is nowhere more than two or three miles wide, and is bounded on either side by precipitous hills of slate and sandstone. In the northeast corner of Section 31, the water-worn material of the kame gives place to till, which contains many granitic pebbles a foot or more in diameter. In crossing the head of the Scioto Valley, on a road running east and west through this point, three parallel ridges are encountered, running nearly north and south, each one in order toward the river extending farther south.

SPRINGFIELD TOWNSHIP.

About halfway between Hopetown, in Springfield township, and Chillicothe the first terrace (over which the railroad runs) is about a half mile in width. The second terrace, which occupies the remaining space to the hills on the east, which is also about a half mile in width, rises abruptly 48 feet above the river.

UNION TOWNSHIP.

In driving up the Scioto, upon the west side, from Chilli" cothe, the road follows the first terrace, which is about a mile wide, and 20 feet above the river. Kame-like ridges appear in Union township, nearly opposite the southwest corner of Green, and just above the second toll-gate, where the Clarkson pike branches off to the west. The cross-road leading directly west from this point ascends 400 feet (B) in the first mile. Granitic boulders are abundant at this elevation, and a well one-half mile south passes 33 feet through what was called "gravel," but is doubtless "till." Granitic boulders appear upon this plateau for a half mile or so farther south. The till is of great depth, one-half mile north of the centre, on the farm of J. A. Hurst. From the centre, southwest, past the houses of M. A. Pinto and W. R. Bowdle, to the Frankfort pike, the road continues upon the highlands, and passes many granitic boulders, and through occasional deposits of till, but the till is not deep. There is considerable development of till at the cross-road near the house of Susan Beard, and again, upon descending the hill to the turnpike near the house of Jacob Flescher; but no till appears along the pike to the west for a mile, where, upon descending about 150 feet, the road enters, at about 150 feet above the north fork of Paint Creek and about a mile and a half east of Frankfort in Concord township, a deposit of till which is unbroken to the north and northwest. The railroad from Chillicothe to Roxabel strike into extensive drift deposits at Anderson's, upon the north fork of Paint, which is specially abundant at Musselman's.

The deposit here is at least 25 or 30 feet deep, and looks like till, though the material is very fine.

One-half mile south of Musselman's, upon the Greenfield pike, in Twin township, there is a small deposit of till, near the school-house, upon the farm of C. C. Plyley. The road is here 550 feet (B) above Chillicothe, and continues at this height west to Lattaville, in Concord township. A mile east of Lattaville, a well upon the farm of J. McConnell passed through 12 feet yellow clay, 3 or 4 feet blue clay, 10 feet yellow clay, 5 feet gravel. About 13 feet from the top a piece of wood 3 or 4 feet long and 3 inches through was found in clay. From this point the eye surveys a vast extent of till in the valley of the North Fork of Paint, which is about 400 feet lower. But the hills facing the north are here completely enveloped in till. The ice seems for a long while to have crowded down to this rocky escarpment, and for a short time to have overlapped it upon both sides of the North Fork.

Lattaville, in Concord township, is built upon a striking development of the moraine. The turnpike follows the moraine across the southeast corner of Concord township. The general elevation is from 150 to 200 feet above the valley of the creek, while knolls and ridges of till rise 50 or 60 feet higher. About one mile south is the continuation of the rocky hills 200 or 300 feet higher, through which the North Fork of Paint Creek has cut its way below Frankfort. One mile south of Lattaville till and many granitic boulders appeared near T. M. McDonald's, upon the very summit of the plateau, 625 feet (B) above Chillicothe. A mile southwest, upon the other side of the watershed, in the upper valley of Lower Twin Creek, there is a small amount of till near the school-house. South and east of this to the valley of Paint Creek there is no more till. There are some remarkable kames and terraces in these two townships which deserve notice. As we have said, the North Fork of Paint Creek, above Frankfort, flows through a broad expanse of glaciated country everywhere enveloped in till and dotted with granitic boulders. Two miles southeast, near Musselman's, it enters a narrow valley about 400 feet deep, and a half mile wide, in which it continues for about 5 miles ; when it comes out into a broader valley, and flows southeast until it unites with the Scioto below Chillicothe.   Before the river enters this gorge separating Union from Twin Township, the valley is marked by numerous kame-like ridges, running nearly parallel with the stream.   Between Frankfort and Roxabel numerous kettle holes appear.   One and a half mile south of Frankfort, on the south side of a small tributary to the creek, is a kame 57 feet above the general level of the valley.   Granitic pebbles are numerous in this.   One near the summit measured 3 feet. This kame runs at least three-fourths of a mile to the southeast.   Upon emerging from the gorge below Frankfort, in the eastern angle of Twin township, between Paint Creek and North Fork, extensive kames are found to connect the two valleys along the line of Cat Tail Run.   The material in these kames is water-worn, and ranges from pebbles of granite 2 feet through to fine sand.   Granitic boulders 3 feet through occur on the top of the gravel ridges.   These ridges are more than 180 feet high, and descend upon each side at an angle of 25 or 30 degrees.   Near the residence of Captain Phill. A. Rodes, facing Paint Creek, near the outlet of Wilcox Run, the kame is 158 feet high, and encircles a kettle-hole of great dimensions.

It is very clear, as Professor Orton surmised (see Geological Survey of Ohio, vol. II, p. 653), that Paint Creek, in preglacial times, passed northward, and joined the North Fork, near the eastern angle of Twin township ; but in glacial times that outlet was obstructed by ice, and partly filled with gravel, so that the creek left its broad valley, and has cut a channel for three miles across the rocky escarpment, which here formerly separated it from the Scioto.   This post-glacial channel, which it now occupies, is "not more than 200 feet in width at the base, is bottomed with rock, and is bounded by precipitous cliffs not less than 300 feet in height.   After following a southeast course for three miles, it turns again to the northeast, and regains its old valley two miles west of the south line of Chillicothe."

From the fact that the old valley of Paint Creek is filled only to about one-third the height of the surrounding hills, it seems clear that the ice-front itself rested over the eastern angle Twin township long enough for the creek to wear the gorge just described to nearly its present depth. Perhaps this would require 2,000 or 3,000 years.

BUCKSKIN TOWNSHIP.

The boundary of the deep accumulation of till enters Buckskin township a half mile or more south of the Greenville pike, and crosses in a pretty direct line to Paint township, one-half mile or more south of Salem. The road from the Greenville pike, near Henry Parrett's, to Salem, leads over a continuous deposit of till thrown up into low hills and ridges. The rocky escarpment extending from the Scioto River through Union and Twin township, crosses Buckskin township about a mile and a half southeast of Salem. We did not ascend it in this township, but from what we have described in Twin township, and from what we shall describe in Paint township, it is probable that the ice-sheet overlapped these hills, which are all along from 400 to 500 feet above the land to the north.

PAINT TOWNSHIP.

With the exception of the northwestern corner, Paint township consists of sandstone ridges left from the erosion of a continuous plateau, which was from 500 to 550 feet (B) above the valley of Paint Creek at Bainbridge. The ice surmounted these summits, and left considerable deposits of till and granitic boulders upon them, near the residence of D. H. Pricer, 3 miles south of Salem, and at various places along the ridge road south to Bainbridge as far as Henry Benner's. Near D. H. Pricer's, at an elevation of 550 feet (B) above Bainbridge, was a boulder of hornblendic rock, about 5x3x2 feet. Many boulders 2½ feet through appeared at this elevation farther south.

PAXTON TOWNSHIP.

No till was observed in Paxton township, except near the woolen factory on Buckskin Creek, whence it appears at intervals both on the road leading up the creek to the north,

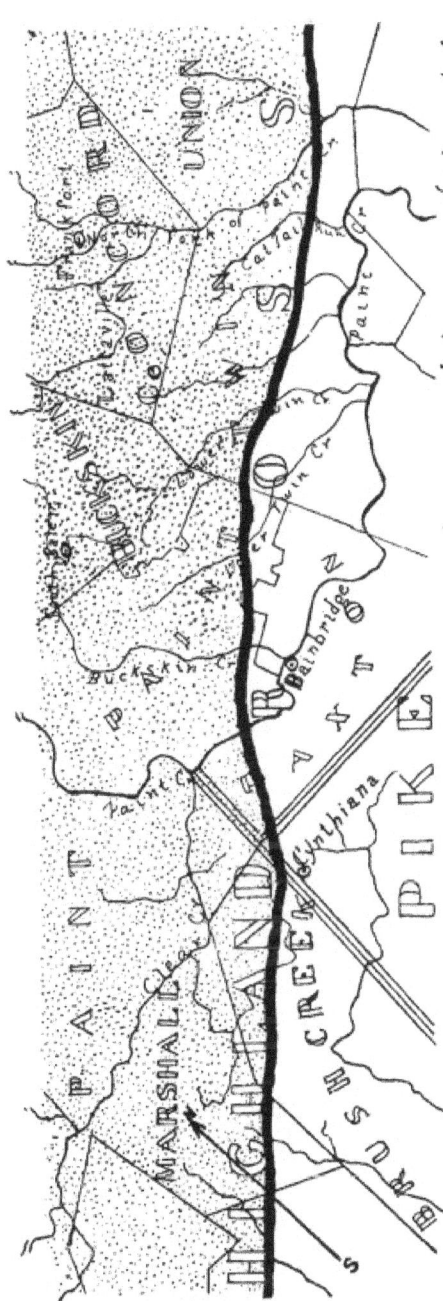

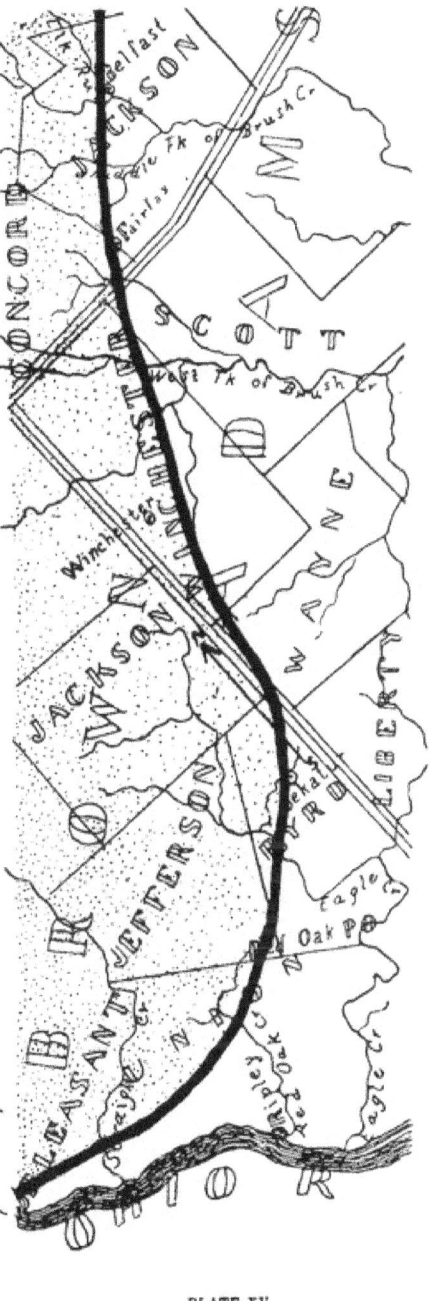

PLATE XIV.

PLATE XV.

and also on the road to the right, leading upon the hill along which we marked the line of till and boulders in Paint township. A little till also appears in the northwestern corner of the town, near Rocky Fork.

Bainbridge is in a valley about a mile wide, which has been cut down through parallel strata of sand rock and shale to a depth of about 500 feet. The village is built upon a terrace whose surface is about 25 feet above high-water mark. The material varies from coarse sand to well-rounded pebbles 4 or 5 inches through. Limestone prevails, though granite is also present. A granitic boulder 4 feet in diameter was observed. One mile west of Bainbridge the terrace rises suddenly 15 feet. Just below the junction of Rock Fork till appears in small hillocks. The elevation is 125 feet (B) above Bainbridge. From this point to Hillsboro, in Highland county, signs of glaciation are continuous.

PIKE COUNTY.

Following south from Paint Creek, along the Ross county line, till disappears suddenly one-quarter of a mile north of Cynthiana, in the extreme northwest corner of Pike county. To the west and southwest till is abundant.

HIGHLAND COUNTY.

The boundary enters Highland county, near the northeast corner of Brush Creek township, and continues, in a southwest direction to Marshall township, about one mile north of its southeast corner. The deposits are continuous along the road from Cynthiana to Carmel post office, south southwest to the school-house by J. West's, near the head of the middle fork of Brush Creek, and three-quarters of a mile south of the road from Sinking Spring to Marshall. To the southeast of this line across Brush Creek township, there are hills of sand rock and shale of great height. On the east side of these hills, two miles south of Carmel post office, near the residence of D. W. Scammahorn, there is, however, an extensive deposit of till, which continues on the road south nearly to Baker's Fork, but there disappears. From this point around to Cynthiana no till was observed.

MARSHALL TOWNSHIP.

There are heavy deposits of till all over the northern part of Marshall township. It is specially abundant south and west of the village, with many granitic boulders 3 and 4 feet in diameter. Towards the southeast part of the town the spaces upon which there is no till are extensive. But at the corner, by Jacob Kesler's, is a small deposit of till, with granitic boulders. There is none upon the road east to Brush Creek, and none south to Jackson township. The distance from each of these townships is about a mile. But a half mile west from Mr. Kesler's an extensive and deep deposit of till begins, and is continuous to the west for at least a mile.

JACKSON TOWNSHIP.

The moraine may be said to enter Jackson township one mile northwest of North Uniontown. Upon the road from Marshall to Belfast till is continuous to the west branch of Elk Run, and on the road from Uniontown to Belfast there is no till for two miles. Upon descending to Elk Run, near R. B. Matthew's, granitic pebbles appeared at an elevation of 50 feet above the bridge. Upon ascending the west bank there were occasional appearances of till all along, which, at the cemetery, near J. Weaver's, one-half mile northeast of Belfast, was very abundant. From Belfast, upon the pike towards Hillsboro, saw no till for three miles ; but there was an occasional boulder, one of which, a mile north of the township line, was between 3 and 4 feet in diameter. North of this, till was continuous. West of Belfast no till appeared in the valley of Brush Creek ; but two miles northwest, near Joseph McCoy's, was a considerable deposit of till. Granitic pebbles occurred upon the ridge a mile farther south, near the school-house, by Mrs. Phoela Ford's. This is at an elevation of 600 feet (B) above Cincinnati, and 400 feet (B) above Belfast. On the Ridge road from here to Newmarket there was scarcely any till, but scattered granitic pebbles. The elevation is between 600 and 700 feet (B) above Cincinnati. From Newmarket there was a continuous sheet of till, in places very deep.

Along the town line south of Fairfax to Adams county there is a continuous and extensive accumulation of till at an elevation of 650 feet above Cincinnati. Upon the road running southeast from Fairfax granitic boulders are occasionally found for three-quarters of a mile, but beyond that are absent, and no more could be found upon the east side of Rocky Run.

ADAMS COUNTY.

The boundary line of the glaciated region enters Adams county in the northwest corner of Scott township, near the line between Concord and Jackson townships, in Highland county. Between Winchester Post Office and Mount Lee the till is nearly continuous, though not deep. The west fork of Brush Creek is remarkably free from drift material, and no till appears upon the road from Mount Lee to North Liberty. On the railroad from Winchester to Youngsville, on the east side of Elk Run, two miles from Winchester, is a cut in till from 10 to 20 feet in depth. Angular granitic boulders are found near here from 2½ to 3 feet through. On the road northwest from North Liberty large deposits of till occur, near Elk Run, two miles southeast of Winchester Village. The deposit was from 5 to 20 feet in depth. In driving from Winchester to Eckmansville, on the south border of Wayne township, till is continuous to within a mile of Eckmansville, where it disappears. On turning southwest from Eckmansville, across the northwest corner of Liberty township, the deposit of till is re-entered near the county line.

BROWN COUNTY.

On the road from Eckmansville to Ripley till is continuous through Byrd township. Two miles and a-half southwest of Decatur, near the Christian Church, and not far from Jefferson Post Office, is a granitic boulder 2 or 3 feet through. Till continued to Red Oak Post Office, in Jefferson township. The road from here to Ripley descended through a gorge 450 feet deep. Found some small pebbles upon the summit of the hills north of Ripley; also, in Lewis township, upon the summit of the hills, 2 miles north of Higginsport, found thin deposits of

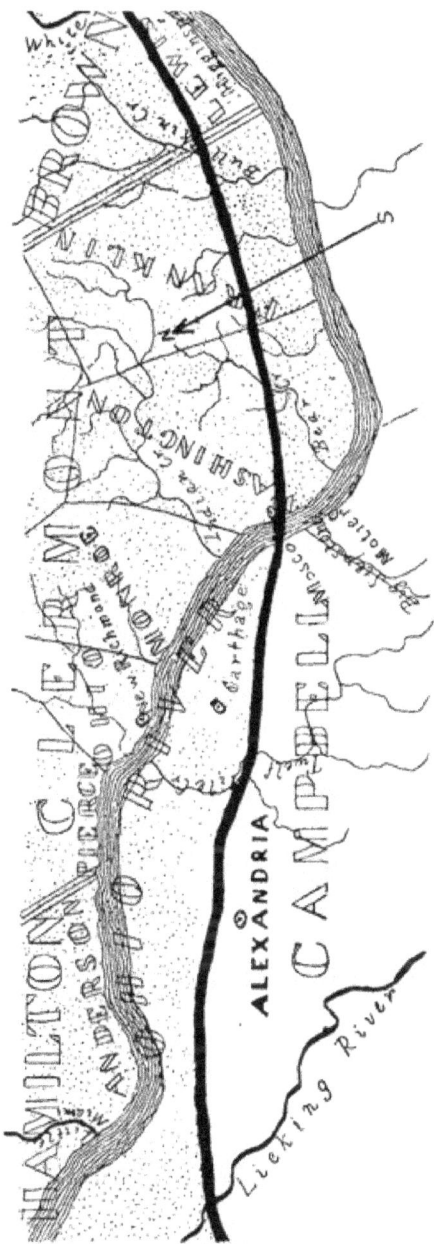

PLATE XVI.

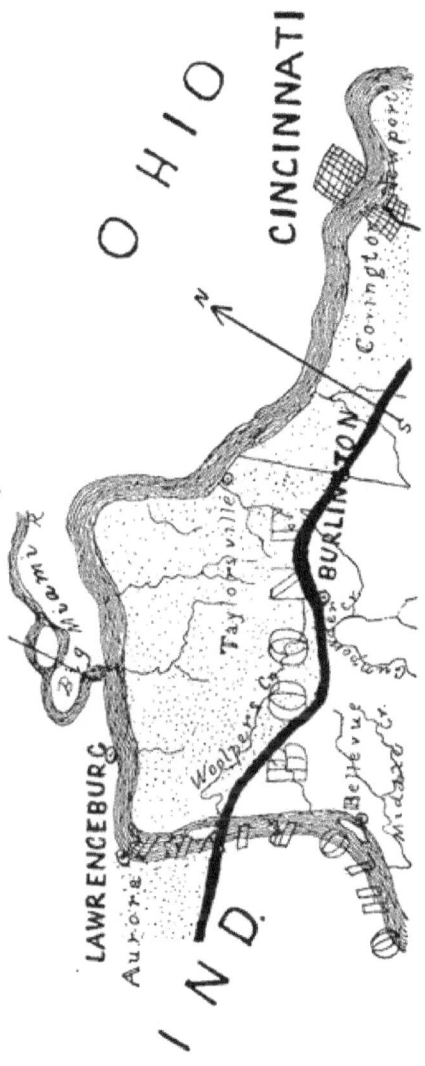

PLATE XVII.

till. A granitic boulder, measuring 3½x2½, and 1½ feet out of
ground, was found in a small brook about half way up these
hills.   Franklin and Washington townships, in Clermont
county, I have not examined, but I presume the glacial boundary approaches pretty close to the river. (See remarks below
upon Kentucky.) Mr. Charles W. Smith informs me that
there are small granitic boulders on the high lands two or
three miles northeast of Ripley, and that on the highest hills
in Ohio, opposite Augusta, Ky., pebbles of diorite and jasper
are abundant ; but diligent search upon the Kentucky hills,
near Augusta, disclosed nothing but local *debris* of the stratified rocks of the region, except an occasional quartz pebble as
large as the end of one's finger.

HAMILTON COUNTY.

At Walnut Hill Station is an extensive deposit of till from
10 to 20 feet in depth.   Scratched stones and small granitic
fragments are abundant in it.   This is about 350 feet above
the river.   At North Bend the Cincinnati, Indianapolis and
St. Louis Railroad passes from the valley of the Ohio to the
valley of the Miami by a tunnel, through an extensive deposit
of till.   The height of this deposit above low water-mark is
upwards of 160 feet.   No large granitic pebbles were seen in
it, but the examples of striated pebbles were numerous and
excellent.   Below North Bend the space between the Ohio
and the Miami is occupied by a remnant of the limestone
plateau through which the rivers have worn their present
deep channels.   This is 375 or 400 feet (B) above the river,
and is about 4 miles long and 2 miles wide.   Till and granitic
pebbles 2 feet through are found upon this summit.   They
are also found in Indiana upon the summit, of equal height
to the west and southwest, across the broad valleys of the
Miami and the White Water.

KENTUCKY.

The glacial boundary enters Kentucky in CAMPBELL
COUNTY, crossing the Ohio River about two miles north of
the Pendleton county line. I have not examined sufficiently
the northern part of Campbell county, and I can only fix the
limit near the river. We crossed the river from New Richmond, in Ohio, and ascended through the channel of a small
brook to the summit of the Kentucky hills, near Carthage.
These hills are about four hundred feet above the river, and
the ascent is very steep. Granitic pebbles were numerous in
the bed of this small stream, and, upon reaching the summit,
we found the surface covered with till to the depth of ten or
fifteen feet, in which granitic boulders a foot through were
numerous, and in which it was not difficult to find beautiful
specimens of scratched stones. From this point we went
south, keeping upon the summit of the plateau from one and
a half to three miles from the river. Indications of glacial
action continued, but in a somewhat diminishing degree,
until reaching Flag's Spring, where they ceased entirely.
But to make sure, we went on in the same direction about
four miles farther, and came down to the river at Motier,
without seeing any farther glacial marks. At Flag's Spring
there is an extensive accumulation of post-glacial conglomerate like that at Split Rock, soon to be described.

KENTON COUNTY.

My examination of Kenton county has been too brief to be
very satisfactory, but what I have seen may serve as a guide to
others. Three miles southwest of Covington the hills are
covered with loam from 15 to 40 feet deep, at an elevation of 400 feet (B) above the river. There are occasional
small quartz pebbles in this loam ; but I saw no sure signs of
the actual presence of ice. In my notes I have said : "This
seems like the bottom of a temporary lake when the ice
dammed the river below." On going across from the pike a
little south of this, so as to strike the Licking River, two miles

south of Covington flats, no glacial marks were observed. At
Erlanger, however, the first station south of Ludlow, on the Cincinnati Southern Railroad, a railroad cut shows clay to a depth
of six feet or more containing pebbles of quartzite, limestone,
and occasionally granite, near the bottom.   All, however,
were small, none of them more than three inches in diameter.
The elevation is about five hundred feet above the river.

BOONE COUNTY.

The glacial deposits over the northern part of Boone county
are unmistakable in character.   On ascending the hill along
the line of the Covington and Petersburg pike from Ludlow
to Hebron, we encountered about one mile east of Hebron,
and about 450 feet (B) above the river, a deposit of till, twelve
or more feet of which in depth is exposed by a little stream
running to the north.   The whole surface of the country
about Hebron is covered with a loamy deposit containing occasional scratched stones and granitic boulders.   On ascending
the hill from Taylorsville to Hebron small granitic boulders
abound all along the bed of the little stream, and are found of
considerable size in the clay upon the summit.   On the pike
between Florence and Burlington, and two miles west of Burlington, where a small tributary of Gunpowder Creek, which
runs to the south, crosses the pike, a large number of granitic
boulders are collected, they having been washed out of the till
which caps the hills.   The elevation above the river is 400
feet (B).   Three-fourths of a mile to the east the elevation is
575 feet (B), and the headwaters of this tributary, a mile and
a half or two miles north, near Hebron, are 500 feet (B.)   I
counted within a few rods of each other 15 granitic boulders,
one of which measured 2½ feet in diameter.   There were three
or four boulders composed of metaphoric conglomerate, containing the beautiful red jasper pebbles characteristic of the
eastern shore of Lake Superior, and of the region north of
Lake Huron.   They are identical in composition with boulders that are scattered over Michigan, Northern Indiana, and
with one in the Oberlin Museum, found by Professor Allen
in Brownhelm.   Colonel Whittlesey brought a mass of this

rock from its native ledge, near Lake Superior, on the west side of St. Mary's River, and has adorned the yard in front of his residence with it. These boulders in Kentucky are found about five miles south of the Ohio River, and south of the watershed in that part of the county.

In a drive from Petersburg to Hebron, the hills were found to be covered with till to a height of several hundred feet. The barometer read about 400 feet above the river. The redness of the soil was everywhere noticeable, showing that the iron was thoroughly oxidized. A detour to the south, from Florence to Union, and from Union across Gunpowder Creek, towards Bellevue (now called Grant P. O.), demonstrated the absence of glacial deposits until reaching the headwaters of Middle Creek, about half way between Burlington and Bellevue. Here the tops of the hills are covered with a gravelly deposit, containing occasional granitic pebbles several inches in diameter. Near the headwaters of the southern branches of Middle Creek, and especially at Rock Spring, the deposits are of very coarse material, are of great extent, and are cemented together by an infiltration of lime like that already spoken of at Flag's Spring, and soon to be described at Split Rock. This conglomerate consists largely of pebbles of limestone, but contains also granitic pebbles. It was noticed as early as 1845 by Professor Locke, and described in the Cincinnati *Gazette*, and more recently by Dr. Sutton, of Aurora, who specially notices its great elevation above the river. Dr. Sutton's paper may be found in the proceedings of the A. A. A. S. for 1876, and reprinted, with additional information by Prof. E. T. Cox, in the Geological Survey of Indiana for 1878, pp. 108-113.

The most accessible place in which to study this deposit is near the mouth of Woolper Creek, about four miles northwest of the headwaters of Middle Creek, and about four miles south of Petersburg. The formation is here known as "Split Rock," and rises directly from the Ohio River, both above and below the mouth of Woolper Creek. Professor Locke "regarded this conglomerate as evidence of the destruction of a great arch of rocks which united the coal-fields of Ohio with

those of Indiana and Kentucky." Mr. Robert B. Warder, in
the Geological Report of Indiana, for 1872, also directs attention to this Split Rock conglomerate, and suggests, possibly,
it is the terminal moraine of an ancient glacier. With this
view Dr. Sutton and Professor Cox substantially agree. But
Dr. Sutton and Prof. Cox suppose that the deposits upon the
highland above Middle Creek are far more ancient than those
in the valley of the Ohio about the mouth of Woolper Creek.
As we read the facts, however, now, in the light of the most
recent investigations, these deposits upon the highlands of
Boone county, and at Split Rock, are probably contempora-
neous, the ice of the glacial period extending down to a continuous line which crosses the river at Woolper Creek. The
vast current of water which flowed down at the melting of
the continental glacier, was not determined in its course by
the present channels as now, for these were in many cases
filled with ice, and for a time the southward flowing currents
were borne completely across the channel of the Ohio, flowing
in a trough of ice, whose bottom was as high as the summit of
Boone county.

The pebbles in the cemented mass of Split Rock are mostly
of limestone, and are very coarse—individual pebbles frequently being from three to four feet in diameter. Granitic
pebbles are infrequent. One was found, however, measuring
two feet in diameter. The cliffs of this conglomerate, at the
mouth of Woolper Creek, rise not far from one hundred feet
above the river, and the material is cemented together by an
infiltration of lime. Kame-like ridges extend for two miles
south of Woolper Creek, on the way to Bellevue. These are
composed of rather fine material, and are 160 feet above the
river. The terrace upon this, the Kentucky side of the river,
is, for two miles or more below Woolper Creek, remarkable for
its height, being more than 100 feet above the river, and 56
feet higher than the high-water mark of January, 1883.

APPENDIX.

ABSTRACT OF THE BEARINGS OF GLACIAL STRIÆ AND GROOVES IN OHIO.

COMPILED BY COL. CHARLES WHITTLESEY.

NORTHEASTERN COUNTIES.

ASHTABULA COUNTY—

No observations, the rocks principally shale.

TRUMBULL COUNTY—

Farmington township..............................S. 30° West.
Vernon township........ ....S. 20° 30° and 40° East.
Brookfield ....S. 5° Ea·t.
Over the Pennsylvania line, Shenango Valley...........S. 5° East.
Fowler township ....S. 4°, 30° and 45° East.
Braceville........................... ....S. 45° and 50° West.
Lordstown ....South and S. 20° East.

MAHONING COUNTY LINE—

Austintown...........................S. 30° and 35° East.
Average of four exceptional observations, S. and W. S. 31° West.
Average of ten observations to the East of South, S. 22 4-10° East.

GEAUGA COUNTY—

Thompson......................S. 40° and 50° West, and 50° East.
Hampden.................................S. 10° and 15° East.
Chardon...S. 10° East,
Chester.....................................S. 50° and 70° East.
Russell.....................................S. 50° and 70° East.
Bainbridge........ ....S. 49° East.
Parkman...S. 30° West.

LAKE COUNTY—

Leroy................................ ....S. 45 ° West.

PORTAGE COUNTY—

    Mantua.................................. ....S. 30° and 40° East.

    Four observations W. of South.................Mean S. 41° West.

    Ten observations E, of South.....................S. 37 4·10° East.

CUYAHOGA COUNTY—

    Solon...S. 45° East.

    Euclid..S. 20° and 25° East.

    Independence......................................S. 20° East.

    Average.......................................S 27 1·2° East.

SUMMIT COUNTY—

    Portage near Akron...........................S. 10° to 35° East.

    N. Hampton.................................S. 30° to 60° East.

    N. Hampton.................................S. 30° and 35° East.

    Middlebury, exceptional.........................East and West.

    Tallmadge Coal Hill.........................S. 30° and 40° East.

    Cuyahoga Falls................................ .....S. 45° East.

    Twinsbury...................................S. 40° and 45° East.

MEDINA COUNTY—

    Copley.......................................S. 30° West·

    Sharon..S. 40° East.

WAYNE COUNTY—

    Doylestown.......... ....West and South.

    Average, not anomalous.................... ...S. 36 6-10° East.

WEST END OF LAKE ERIE.

Between Buffalo at the East end of this Lake, and the Islands, the rocks near the water level are generally too soft to retain the ancient ice-markings. On the lime rock at Buffalo, there are numerous and distinct etchings, that bear from South 25° to South 30° West, and run under water. Their bearings are nearly parallel with the axis of the trough of the Lake. At the mouth of Detroit River, near Gibraltar, the limestone beds are grooved and polished, and the bearings are also South 30° West. The Islands, and the limestone shores to the South and West, are everywhere scoured and grooved in the same way; but the bearing is generally more to the West, differing by nearly a right angle with the general bearing in the Northeastern Counties.

KELLEY'S ISLAND AND ADJACENT—

    Southeast corner, at water level, long grooves.........S. 75° West.

    Southeast corner, cross striæ.......................N. 80° West.

    Calkins' Quarry, north side, deep grooves...........S. 80° West.

KELLEY'S ISLAND, AND ADJACENT—*Continued—*

Calkins' Quarry, striæ...............................S. 70° West.
Calkins' Quarry, water level, striæ.................N. 80° West.
Calkins' Quarry, one heavy groove.............. ...S. 45° West.
Calkins' Quarry, one striæ.........................S. 60° West.
Mean of twelve observations in different parts of Island, S. 80° West.
West Sister Island, mean ....S. 80° West·
Put-in-Bay, mean of twenty observations.... ....S. 80° West.
Sandusky City, mean of four observations............S. 78° West.
Sandusky City, mean of two observations............S. 80° West.
Sandusky City, mean of one observation......... ...S. 81° West.

ERIE COUNTY—

Belleville...S. 75° West.
Belleville..S. 65° West.

OTTAWA COUNTY—

Geneva ....S. 65° West.

LUCAS COUNTY—

Sylvanus, five observations.........................S. 50° West.
Monclova, four observations.........................S. 62° West.
Whitehouse...S. 50° West.
Near Maumee River, seven observations.............S. 62° West.

WOOD COUNTY—

Portage, three observations ....S. 50° West.
Otsego, three observations........ ....S. 64° West.
Defiance..S. 45° West.

PAULDING COUNTY—

Junction, three observations........................S. 45° West.

VAN WERT COUNTY—

Middlepoint, two observations.......................S. 15° West.

HANCOCK COUNTY—

Findlay, three observations.........................S. 43° West.

PUTNAM COUNTY—

Blanchard...S. 20° West.
Sugar Creek..S. 50° West.

AUGLAIZE COUNTY—

Auglaize............................ ....S. 48° West.

SENECA COUNTY—

    Seneca...S. 5° East.

    Seneca...S. 23° West.

WYANDOTTE COUNTY—

    Crawford...S. 20° West.

    Crane...S. 5° West.

    Marseilles..S. 10° West

MARION COUNTY—

    Grand Prairie........................... ....North and South.

MIAMI COUNTY—

    Troy................. ....Glaciated surface: bearings not given.

HIGHLAND COUNTY—

    Near Lexington, according to Professor Orton, very marked roches
    moutonnees. Dr. John Locke, in the Second Report of the First
    Geological Survey, 1838, page 230, has given a *fac simile* of pol.
    ished limestone from Light's quarry, near Dayton, Montgomery
    County. It was done by placing a surface block in a ruling ma-
    chine, by which it engraved itself to perfection. The grooves are
    from the 1-40 to the $\frac{1}{5}$ of an inch deep, and from a line to $\frac{1}{4}$ of an inch
    wide. Both the grooves and the finer striæ are in groups, or fas-
    cicles, as high as ten in number. They were perfectly straight, and
    covered by two feet of earth. The average bearing is about S. 26°
    East, ranging from 19° to 21°, 31° and 33°; but the greater number
    of the most pronounced are S. 26° East.

The above abstract is compiled from the observations of Professors
Newberry, Read, Winchell, and Gilbert of the Second Ohio Survey, and
from those of Colonel Whittlesey. Most of the irregular and exceptional
bearings can be accounted for by the local topography turning aside the
general movement. The highest elevations are 625 to 650 feet above the
Lake, above which the ice sheet must have risen several hundred feet.

EFFECTS OF THE GLACIAL DAM AT CIN-CINNATI ALONG THE UPPER BASIN OF THE OHIO.

BY PROFESSOR I. C. WHITE,

OF THE PENNSYLVANIA GEOLOGICAL SURVEY.

Among the papers read before the geological section at the recent meeting of the American Association for the Advancement of Science at Minneapolis, 1883, was the following by Professor I. C. White, of the University of West Virginia, on the *Glacial Dam* at Cincinnati, and the evidences of the West Virginia portion of the vast lake made by that dam :

"In a paper read before the Boston Society of Natural History, March 7, 1883, Rev. G. F. Wright has shown that the southern rim of the great northern ice-sheet crossed the Ohio River, near the site of New Richmond, a few miles above Cincinnati. Mr. Wright believes that one effect of this invasion of the Ohio Valley by the glacial ice, was to form an immense dam of ice and morainic *debris* 500 or 600 feet high, which, effectually closed the old channel way, and set back the water of the Ohio and its tributaries, until rising to the level of the Licking River divide, it probably found an outlet through Kentucky around the glacial dam. As this divide is 500 or 600 feet higher than the present bed of the Ohio at Cincinnati, Mr. Wright states that the site of Pittsburgh would have been submerged to the depth of 300 feet, and adds: It remains to be seen how much light this may shed upon the terraces which mark the Ohio and its tributaries in Western Pennsylvania.

"Having resided for nearly a score of years in the valley of the Monongabela River, the writer is necessarily familiar with its terraces and surface deposits in general ; and in reply to the above query of the eminent glacialist, would answer that his admirable work throws a flood of light upon the Monongahela terraces, and proffers for them and the deposits along other tributaries of the Ohio, the only satisfactory explantion that has ever been advanced.

"Of course, if the Ohio River was ever so obstructed for any considerable period of time, it would follow, as a necessary result, that many of the tributary streams and the Ohio itself above the limit of the dam, would have their old valleys silted up with vast heaps of trash—clay, sand, gravel, boulders, drifted logs and other rubbish—carried down by the streams from the region not sheeted with ice, and dumped into the great inland lake stream which extended from Cincinnati far up toward the sources of the Monongahela.

"That the valley of the latter stream has been refilled with trash during some period of its history to a height of 250 or 300 feet above its present bed, the evidence is most conclusive, for the remnants of this deposit still cover the surface to a great depth in long lines of terraces extending from Pittsburgh, Pa , southward along the river to Fairmount, W. Va., a distance of 130 miles, and very probably much further, as I have never examined the river valley above the latter town.

"The striking peculiarity of these terrace deposits is that they suddenly disappear at an elevation of 1050 or 1075 feet above tide, not a single rounded and transported boulder ever being found above the latter horizon, though occurring in countless numbers below this level.

"The hills along the river often rise 300 or 400 feet higher than the upper limit of the deposits, so that there can be no mistake about the elevation at which the terrace deposits disappear. The composition of these great heaps of surface *debris* is, along the immediate valley of the river, a heterogeneous mixture of sand, clay, gravel, rounded boulders of sandstone of every size, from an inch in diameter up to four feet, pieces of coal, leaves, logs of wood, and every other species of rubbish usually transported by streams. Back from the channel of the river, however, and especially where the surface configuration would make quiet water, there occur thick deposits of very fine, bluish white clay, in which great numbers of leaves are most beautifully preserved. These clays have been extensively used for the manufacture of pottery at Geneva and Greensboro, Pa., and also to some extent at Morgantown and Fairmount, W. Va. Though the clay deposits occur at nearly every horizon, they are purest near the upper limit of the terraces, and these are consequently the only ones that have hitherto been much explored.

"In the vicinity of Morgantown, terraces of transported material occur at the following approximate (measured by barometer) elevations :

	Ft. above river.	Ft. above tide.
First Terrace	30	820
Second Terrace	75	865
Third Terrace	175	965
Fourth Terrace	200	990
Fifth Terrace	275	1065

"The first terrace is the present flood-plain of the river, consisting principally of fine sand, mud and gravel. It seems to possess some respectable antiquity, however, since Mr. Walter Hough, one of my students, dug some teeth and bones from five feet below its top, which were identified by Professor O. C. Marsh, as the remains of a species of peccary, an animal that has not inhabited the region in question within the American historic epoch.

"All of the other terraces have thick deposits of transported material, wherever the original contour of the surface has favored its preservation from erosion. From the top of the fourth terrace Mr. Keck dug a well through 70 feet of clay, gravel and boulders without finding bed rock. He also encountered logs of wood in a soft or semi-rotten condition near the bottom.

"Many other wells on the third terrace have been sunk to depths of 20 and 30 feet without reaching bed rock.

"The fifth terrace of this Morgantown series marks the height to which the pre-glacial valley of the Monongahela was silted up, partially or entirely during the existence of the glacial dam at Cincinnati, since, as already stated, no clay beds, rounded boulders, or other transported material are ever found above its top, but instead only angular fragments of the country rock, and thin coverings of surface material which has accumulated *in situ.*

"Owing to the considerable elevation—275 feet—of the fifth terrace above the present river bed, its deposits are frequently found far inland from the Monongahela, on tributary streams. A very extensive deposit of this kind occurs on a tributary one mile and a half northeast of Morgantown, and the region, which includes three or four square miles, is significantly known as the 'flats.' The elevation of the 'flats' is 275 feet above the river, or 1065 feet above tide. The deposits on this area consist almost entirely of clays and fine sandy material, there being very few boulders intermingled. The depth of the deposit is unknown, since a well sunk on the land of Mr. Baker passed through alternate beds of clay, fine sand, and muddy trash to a depth of 65 feet without reaching bed rock. In some portions of the clays which make up this deposit, the leaves of our common forest trees are found most beautifully preserved. Whether or not they show any variations from the species growing in that region, the writer has not yet had time to determine, but when a larger collection has been obtained, this subject will receive the attention that it deserves, since if the date of the glacial epoch be very remote, the species must necessarily show some divergence from the present flora.

"Of animal remains the only fragment yet discovered in this highest of the terraces is the tooth of a mastodon, dug up near Stewartstown, seven miles northeast from Morgantown.

"The other tributaries of the Monongahela, on which the writer has noted the clay and other deposits of the fifth terrace, are Decker, Dunkard, Whitely, Muddy, and Ten Mile creeks, and in each case the deposits disappear at the same absolute level at which they cease along the river.

"The Great Kanawha River, another principal tributary of the Ohio, draining a region that was never glaciated, also exhibits water-worn boulder deposits which disappear at 200 to 300 feet above the present level of that stream, though I have not determined the exact limit.

"The glacial dam at Cincinnati presents a complete explanation for the origin of Teazes valley, an ancient, deserted river channel 20 miles long and one or two miles wide, which leaves the Great Kanawha 15 miles below Charleston, W. Va., at Scary, and passing through Putnam and Cabell counties, extends to the valley of Mud River, a tributary of the Guyandotte, which empties into the Ohio at Huntington.

"This valley, although having an elevation of 200 feet or more above the Kanawha, is filled to a great depth with rounded boulders of sandstone, chert, cannel coal, and other trash, which has plainly been trans ported down the Kanawha from above Charleston, so that although it was clearly seen that the water of the Kanawha had once found an outlet to the Ohio by way of this valley and the Mud and Guyandotte rivers, yet why this ancient channel should have been abandoned for the present much more circuitous one had always remained a mystery until Mr. Wright furnished the key in the discovery of the great ice dam at Cincinnati. For it is now clear that such a barrier would set back the water of the Kanawha, until rising above the divide which had previously separated it from Mud River, it sent an arm across to the Ohio by way of the Guyandotte 50 miles below where the other arm and main stream reached the same river at the present mouth of the Kanawha, thus converting portions of Putnam, Mason and Cabell counties into a large, triangular island, the base of which was formed by the swollen Ohio, and the sides by the two arms of the Great Kanawha. The melting away of the Cincinnati dam withdrew the water from the western or Mud-Guyandotte arm of the Kanawha, leaving the abandoned valley high and dry, but littered up with transported trash, as we now see it, while the Kanawha continued on to the Ohio in its present and pre-glacial outlet.

"A summary view of these and other facts in the writer's possession seems to prove, beyond any reasonable doubt, that Mr. Wright's hypothesis concerning the damming up of the Ohio by the glacial ice in the region of Cincinnati was an actual reality ; that during the period of its continuance the principal tributaries of the Ohio had their valleys filled with sediment carried down and dumped into them by the mountain torrents, and other streams which drained the area south from the glaciated region ; that subsequently, when the barrier disappeared, the rivers recut their channels through the silt deposits, probably by spasmodic lowering of the dam, in such a manner as to leave the deposits in a series of more or less regular terraces, which, in favored localities, subsequent erosion has failed to obliterate, though from steep slopes it has removed their every trace.

"The elevation of this dam at Cincinnati, as determined from the upper limit of the fifth Monongahela river terrace, would be somewhere between 1050 feet and 1075 feet above tide, or about 625 feet above low water there in the present Ohio."

Professor White has still more recently (see *The Virginias* for Sept., 1883,) called attention to additional and confirmatory evidence, consisting of small, rounded boulders on the summit of the knob in Sistersville, Tyler county, West Virginia, between five hundred and six hundred feet above the river.

Certain phenomena in Boyd county, Ky., which had been referred to as evidence of direct glacial action I found on examination to be also natural results of the supposed ice dam.

Boyd county is in Northeastern Kentucky, bordering upon West Virginia, and upon the remarkable bend of the Ohio River where it receives the waters of the Big Sandy. Through the attention of Mr. John Campbell of Ironton, O., and Mr. J. H. Means of Ashland, Ky., I was assisted in making a pretty thorough examination of the region. Upon going back about two miles into Kentucky from the Ohio River, opposite Ironton, we find ourselves in a valley two miles wide, running parallel with the Ohio River, and two hundred and twenty feet above it. This valley extends for many miles, reaching the river towards the west at Greenup, and continuing some miles, at least, above Ashland. It is known as Flat Woods. The level is remarkably uniform; and the hills upon either side of it rise about two hundred feet, with numerous lateral openings toward the Ohio. When upon the farther side, and looking northward, one sees the rocky bluffs of the old channel rising so like those facing the river itself that he can scarcely resist the illusion that he is in the present valley of the stream. The supposed glacial phenomena consist of numerous water-worn pebbles of quartz and quartzite scattered along the whole range of this old valley. Most of the pebbles are small, and perfectly rounded, though some were a foot or more in diameter; and one observed was about two feet and a half through, and only slightly worn. These pebbles are not found upon the hills back from this channel, on the Kentucky side, nor, according to Mr. Campbell, who is a most competent witness, anywhere in Lawrence county, O., back from the river. Plainly enough they are the result of water-transportation. Whether they were deposited at the very early period when the Ohio flowed at the level of two hundred and twenty feet higher than now, and regularly occupied this old channel, or whether they were brought into place during the existence of the glacial dam which I have supposed at Cincinnati, I will not venture to say; though the latter theory would seem more in accordance with the facts

published by Professor White concerning the old channel followed by
the Chesapeake and Ohio railroad, extending from the Kanawha River
to the mouth of the Guyandotte in West Virginia. The elevation of the
Kanawha-Guyandotte channel is nearly the same as that of the one I am
describing, and this seems to be a prolongation of that. At any rate,
the pebbles can only be indirectly referred to glacial action, and would
be a very natural result of my theoretical ice dam at Cincinnati.

In *Science* for Sept. 28, 1883, Mr. G. H. Squier describes some phenomena observed by him in the valley of the Licking and its larger
tributaries in Kentucky which had independently, though on less direct
evidence, led him to the same conclusions with myself as to the existence
of an ice dam near Cincinnati. Mr. Squier has kindly furnished me
in a private letter many additional facts for which I gladly give him
credit.

In Bath county he found over an extensive region of low table land,
between Slate Creek and Licking River, and for some distance to the
north, large numbers of water-worn pebbles, composed of white quartz,
chert, black shale and sandstone, and most remarkable of all, fragments of
water-worn coal. These are spread not only over the low table land and in
the valleys, but over the lower hills; but do not extend vertically as high
as the watershed. The pebbles of sandstone and coal must have been
brought down the streams at least twenty miles, and it is evident that
they could not have been left upon this table land and these low hills
by running water. The Cincinnati ice dam supposed would furnish
the required conditions by making a temporary lake into which floating
ice from the east could bring and deposit the materials in the situations
indicated. To use Mr. Squier's own words, "The general level of the
area near the junction of Slate Creek and Licking River is so low that,
save a few hills, it must have all been overflowed [during the existence of
such an ice dam] and the great body of floating ice from above must,
of necessity, have passed directly across it. "So strongly did the above
facts point to a temporary damming of the river, that even in the face
of what I regarded as improbable I was led to the conclusion that the
glacier must have crossed the Ohio."

In the same number of *Science* (Sept. 28) Professor Lesley publishes a
letter in which he speaks of this dam as "furnishing precisely the explanation we need for the *local drift* terraces of the Monongahela and the
rolled northern drift terraces of the lower Allegheny, Beaver, and upper
Ohio rivers."

www.ingramcontent.com/pod-product-compliance
Lightning Source LLC
Chambersburg PA
CBHW031451270326
41930CB00007B/949

9 7 8 3 3 3 7 1 2 5 6 4 6